MENTAL
HEALTH
ISSUES

Catherine Jackson
with Jeannie and Gordon;
Ellen and Bob, Jenny and Daniel;
Angela and David, Charlotte and Jack;
and Abby and Jim, Harry and April.

D1388875

Published by
British Association for Adoption & Fostering
(BAAF)
Saffron House
6–10 Kirby Street
London EC1N 8TS
www.baaf.org.uk

Charity registration 275689 (England and Wales)
and SC039337 (Scotland)

British Library Cataloguing in Publication Data
A catalogue record for this book is available from the British Library

ISBN 978 1 907585 43 2

Project management by Jo Francis, Publications Department, BAAF
Designed and typeset by Fravashi Aga
Printed in Great Britain by the Lavenham Press

BAAF is the leading UK-wide membership organisation for all those
concerned with adoption, fostering and child care issues.

Contents

Acknowledgements

With many, many thanks to the families who agreed to be
interviewed for this book, who freely gave me so much of their time
and shared with us their wisdom gained from personal experience.
Thanks also to Florence Merredew, Health Group Development
Officer at BAAF, for her input.

Note about the author

Catherine Jackson is a freelance writer and editor specialising in
mental health and social care.

The series editor

The editor of this series, **Hedi Argent**, is an established author/editor
for BAAF. Her books cover a wide range of family placement topics;
she has written several guides and a story book for young children.

Looking behind the label…

Jack has mild learning difficulties and displays some characteristics of ADHD and it is uncertain whether this will increase…

Beth and Mary both have a diagnosis of global developmental delay…

Abigail's birth mother has a history of substance abuse. There is no clear evidence that Abigail was prenatally exposed to drugs but her new family will have to accept some kind of developmental uncertainty…

Jade has some literacy and numeracy difficulties, but has made some improvement with the support of a learning mentor…

Prospective adopters and carers are often faced with the prospect of having to decide whether they can care for a child with a health need or condition they know little about and have no direct experience of. No easy task…

Will Jack's learning difficulties become more severe?
Will Beth and Mary be able to catch up?
When will it be clear whether or not Abigail has been affected by parental substance misuse?
And will Jade need a learning mentor throughout her school life?

It can be difficult to know where to turn for reliable information. What lies behind the diagnoses and "labels" that many looked after children bring with them? And what will it be like to live with them? How will they benefit from family life?

Parenting Matters is a unique series, "inspired" by the terms used – and the need to "decode them" – in profiles of children needing new permanent families. Each title provides expert knowledge about a particular condition, coupled with facts, figures and guidance presented in a straightforward and accessible style. Each book also describes what it is like to parent an affected child, with adopters and foster carers "telling it like it is", sharing their parenting experiences, and offering useful advice. This combination of expert information and first-hand experiences will help readers to gain understanding, and to make informed decisions.

Titles in the series will deal with a wide range of health conditions and steer readers to where they can get more information. They will offer a sound introduction to the topic under consideration and offer a glimpse of what it would be like to live with a "labelled" child. Most importantly, this series will look behind the label and give families the confidence to look more closely at a child whom they otherwise might have passed by.

Keep up with new titles as they are published by signing up to our newsletter on www.baaf.org.uk/bookshop.

Shaila Shah

Introduction

This book is concerned with mental disorders, and the particular needs of children born in families with a history of mental ill health, who may be at greater risk of mental disorders themselves.

The first half of the book starts with a short explanation of mental disorders generally and how mental disorder may manifest in children. It goes on to outline the risk of mental disorder in a child from a family with a history of mental disorder, and the factors (genetic and environmental) that can put these children at greater risk. There is also a short explanation of what is currently known about the physiological processes that may explain a child's behaviours and higher vulnerability to mental disorder.

There is a known genetic risk of inheriting mental disorder, and an added and independent risk of a child developing a mental disorder if she or he is exposed to physical, emotional or sexual abuse and neglect. There is also a major risk of lasting harm to a child's mental wellbeing, including their cognitive capacities and learning abilities, if they do not receive sensitive and responsive care from their main caregiver in their very early years.

The second half of the book tells the stories of parents who have adopted children with a history of mental disorder in the family (whether known at the time of adoption or not), and how they have coped. The stories in this section describe some very great difficulties and some even greater rewards. The final outcomes may not always be entirely happy, but for these children, who came from very damaging home environments, their new families brought safety, security, consistency and love.

UNDERSTANDING MENTAL HEALTH PROBLEMS

CATHERINE JACKSON

CHAPTER 1

What are mental health problems?

What are mental health problems?

Mental ill health is common. One in four of us will experience a mental health problem of some kind in the course of our life. Among children and young people, one in ten has an emotional or mental health problem, including conduct and behavioural problems.

Some social groups are at higher risk of mental disorder. Research has found that children who are looked after by their local authority have much higher levels of mental health problems and behavioural and conduct disorders than children in foster care and those living with their birth family.

Of all mental health problems, the **common mental health problems** of depression, anxiety, panic attacks, obsessions and phobias are, as their name implies, more common. These affect around 18 per cent of the adult population, but are more common among women (21 per cent) than men (12 per cent). This doesn't sound like a lot, but it adds up – half of all adults are likely to experience at least one episode in their lifetime.

The more **severe mental disorders** – schizophrenia, psychosis and bipolar disorder (also known as manic depression) – occur less frequently and affect just under one in 100 of the adult population.

Personality disorder, which is not strictly a mental health problem but is widely accepted as a mental disorder, is also quite rare. Personality disorders (there are several sub-types) affect an estimated six per cent of men and four per cent of women, although we do not have precise figures as people with these difficulties mostly do not seek help from mental health services.

In addition, **drug and alcohol abuse** are also recognised forms of mental disorder. It is estimated that nearly a quarter of the adult population drink at what are termed "hazardous" levels (enough to put their health at serious risk), and six per cent (nine per cent of men and four per cent of women) are dependent on alcohol. Three per cent of the population are dependent on illegal drugs.

There are particular "**high risk**" **points** in people's lives, for example, the death of someone close, or a life change like moving house or retiring from work. Pregnant women are vulnerable to depression: 13 per cent will experience depression during pregnancy. Depression rates fall to six per cent in the first few months following the birth, but shoot up again to 22 per cent at 12 months. This can have important implications for their child's physical and mental health, development and wellbeing.

Older people are also more vulnerable to depression, particularly if they are in residential or nursing care.

CHAPTER 2

Mental health problems in children and adults

Estimating the prevalence of mental disorder among children is less straightforward than in adults. Children's mental and emotional distress is more likely to manifest in behavioural or conduct difficulties, rather than symptoms that would be given a diagnosis of mental disorder in an adult.

Most mental disorder has its roots in childhood. Half of all adult mental disorders first become apparent before the age of 14, and three-quarters emerge before the middle-20s.

Which mental health problems do children have?

The most common mental disorder in children is **conduct disorder**. About six per cent of children and young people aged 5–16 years have a conduct disorder and 18 per cent have behavioural problems that are not sufficiently severe or long-lasting to meet the threshold for a formal diagnosis. Conduct disorders are more common in boys than in girls. About eight per cent of boys aged 5–16 have a conduct disorder, and four per cent of girls, and these rates increase with age.

Around four per cent of children aged 5–16 years have an **emotional disorder**, such as depression, anxiety, obsessions or phobias.

Rates of **hyperkinesis** or **Attention Deficit Hyperactivity Disorder (ADHD)** – sometimes known as **Attention Deficit Disorder (ADD)** in the US – are between three and five per cent. This disorder is more commonly diagnosed in boys – by a ratio of between two and four to one – and is not necessarily linked to mental ill health.[1]

Other kinds of mental disorder are much rarer. **Eating disorders** are more common in girls and young women, although the number of boys with anorexia or bulimia is increasing. An estimated one per cent of girls and women in the UK aged 15–30 have anorexia nervosa, and between one and two per cent have bulimia nervosa. The average age of onset for eating disorders is 15–18 years. However, a small but significant number of children aged 10 and under (three in every 100,000) have an eating disorder.

Autistic spectrum disorders (ASD) affect one per cent of children, and a similar percentage of adults. Boys are more likely than girls to have an ASD.

Another increasing mental health problem among teenage young people is **self-harm** (as distinct from suicide attempts). As this is frequently, and deliberately, a hidden problem, it is difficult to

---

[1] ADHD and autism will be covered in more detail in forthcoming BAAF publications in this series.

assess its scale. It is estimated that between one in 10 and one in 15 young people aged 11 upwards self-harm on a regular basis. This means, on average, at least two children in every secondary school class are likely to be self-harming. Self-harm includes cutting, burning, hitting, scratching or pulling out hair as well as swallowing toxic substances and overdosing on medications. It mainly occurs in older children and young people, but has been found among children as young as five and seven years.

Often children with one mental health problem have several others. For example, one-third of children diagnosed with a conduct disorder also have anxiety, ADHD or depression or misuse substances.

Which children are more likely to have mental health problems?

Boys are more likely than girls to have a diagnosed mental disorder, and rates across both sexes increase in adolescence. Ten per cent of boys and five per cent of girls aged 5–10 years have a mental disorder; for those aged 11–16 years, the figures are 13 per cent of boys and 10 per cent of girls. Boys are more likely to have a conduct disorder; girls are at higher risk of emotional problems.

Mental health problems are more common among white children in the UK; children of Indian origin have the lowest rates of mental disorders.

While these rates are of concern, they also tell us that most children don't get mental health problems. However, some children are at much greater risk of developing a mental disorder than others.

As noted earlier, children with the highest rates of mental health problems include looked after children (children in local authority care). Other children with a higher risk of mental disorder are those with learning disabilities, children of offenders and children who have been physically, emotionally and/or sexually abused or neglected.

Poverty and learning difficulties (or low IQ) are also very important risk factors for mental disorder in children.

If we can understand what makes a child more vulnerable to mental health problems and behavioural and conduct disorders, we will be better placed to work out what might help, and also understand why our attempts to help may not always be successful. The hard truth is that, for some children, the odds against their being able to overcome the difficulties associated with their backgrounds and birth families are just too high.

The next chapter briefly summarises the different kinds of mental health, behavioural and conduct problems in children and adults, and the range of services and professionals who can help them. This is followed by chapters on the most common risks to a child's mental health and what can protect them; positive parenting and how poor parenting can lead to mental disorders; and findings from neurological research. These findings go some way towards providing an explanation for why some childhood disorders and behaviours are more frequent in abused and neglected children, and why they can be difficult to remedy despite a child's upbringing in a nurturing adoptive or foster care environment.

CHAPTER 3

Mental disorders: diagnoses and treatments

Mental disorders range from the common (depression and anxiety, together or singly) to the severe (schizophrenia and bipolar disorder).

When the symptoms are so severe that they interfere with the person's ability to cope with daily life or they pose a risk to themselves or other people, they can be treated with a range of therapies, including medication.

Common mental disorders

Depression
People often say they are depressed when in fact they mean they are feeling unhappy. Unhappiness is mostly a reaction to a short-term problem or upset and it goes when the problem is resolved or something good happens to cheer the person up. Depression is

11

a much more powerful and long-lasting condition. Depression can occur in response to an external event or trigger, or it can seem to have no identifiable external cause or trigger. It can manifest as persistent low mood that colours the world grey. It can also be very disabling: people with serious depression can find it impossible to get up and face the day. Depression is associated with:

- sleep difficulties and early waking (insomnia);

- not wanting to eat;

- eating too much (comfort eating);

- tiredness for no reason;

- restlessness, agitation and inability to relax;

- over-anxiety and emotional fragility.

There are many different forms of treatment for depression. It is mostly treated in primary care. A GP may prescribe medication: these days, GPs most commonly prescribe SSRIs (selective serotonin reuptake inhibitors), of which fluoxetine is the most effective. Another SSRI, paroxetine, has been associated with suicide risk, and is not recommended in the UK for children and young people aged under 18. Your GP should be able to advise you fully on the risks and side effects. GPs may also refer children and young people for "talking treatments", on their own or in association with medication. These include a range of different approaches, such as counselling, psychotherapy, cognitive behavioural therapy (CBT) and interpersonal therapy (IPT).

Of these, only CBT and IPT have been tested in formal clinical trials and both have been found to be beneficial for treating depression in children and young people. This does not mean that people have not found counselling and psychotherapy (of which there are many different variants) helpful; it is simply that these treatments have not been subject to comparable clinical trials.

It is very important that parents and carers explore the different options carefully and seek expert medical advice. Finding the right treatments for your child may not be easy and certainly won't be quick, and it is likely that help will come from several different approaches, over time and in combination. There is no magic bullet to treat mental disorders.

Some people find alternative and complementary therapies helpful. These include relaxation, yoga, massage and homeopathic or natural herbal remedies. Exercise and sport can alleviate the effects of depression and help recovery, as can gentle and creative activities like gardening and art. Being outdoors in green spaces, or just looking at a lovely landscape, even if only in a picture or through a window, have been shown to boost mental health.

Again, few clinical trials have been conducted on alternative and complementary therapies and it is important to research their use and seek expert medical advice. Some of these treatments are simply ineffective, but a few could be positively harmful.

Getting involved in group activities and social groups can also help by encouraging social interaction and by giving people something meaningful to do. People with depression tend to withdraw from social contact, but social isolation and loneliness can both cause depression and make it worse.

Anxiety

Anxiety is another over-used term. Anxiety is a normal human emotion; it only becomes a problem when it starts to take over your life and you feel disproportionately worried all the time, with no rational reason. People with anxiety can find it hard to concentrate and may lose their temper easily. They may have panic attacks, and feel very stressed in particular situations, so their heart races. They may even get physical chest pains that feel like a heart attack.

Some people have phobias: they may become terrified of going outside (agoraphobia), or of being in small spaces (claustrophobia), or of meeting new people or going to new places. They may have an absolute terror of spiders or other commonplace creatures that effectively prevents them from going out and enjoying a normal life.

Obsessive compulsive disorders (OCD)

People with OCD are driven by fear and anxiety to perform ritualised, repetitive behaviours. They may repeatedly wash their hands or arrange things in a particular order, or do things in a compulsive, ritualised way, such as touch certain objects a set number of times before leaving the house. Even the childhood game of not walking on the cracks between paving stones can become an OCD. Rituals invented with the intention of keeping the person safe, or to avert some catastrophe, can accumulate and multiply until they dominate the person's whole life. People who are obsessive about hygiene will find it difficult to go out because they don't want to touch anything someone else has touched and will worry about being unable to wash their hands.

OCD is usually treated with behaviourial therapy. The person may be encouraged to challenge their fears and gradually reduce their reliance on the ritualised behaviours. Medications like SSRIs may also be prescribed to relieve the anxiety and fear that provoke the obsessive behaviours.

Many people find it helps to talk about their difficulties and coping strategies in self-help groups with others in the same situation. Cognitive behavioural therapy can be effective in helping people test out their fears and escape habitual patterns of response to particular triggers. Some people learn relaxation techniques to help them cope with difficult situations.

SECTION 1

Personality disorders

Our personality is the way we think and feel and behave. Some people think and feel and behave in extreme ways that make it very difficult for them to get on with other people and to cope with ordinary life. They may have trouble controlling their feelings and behaviour and may get very angry and distressed and hurt themselves or other people. They may also struggle to empathise with other people and to understand other people's needs and viewpoints, or they may be so damaged that they deliberately seek to hurt other people.

Personality disorders in adults take a number of forms and are grouped into diagnostic "clusters". The symptoms are exaggerated manifestations of quite ordinary human feelings and behaviours. The clusters are outlined here.

- People with paranoid personality disorder (cluster A) are highly suspicious and mistrustful.

- People with anti-social personality disorder (also cluster A) have no respect for the law or other people's rights and feelings.

- People with narcissistic personality disorder (cluster B) lack empathy and have a driving hunger to be admired.

- People with avoidant personality disorder (cluster C) feel socially inadequate, are terrified of social events, and think everyone has a low opinion of them.

- People with borderline personality disorder (BPD occurs mostly in women, and particularly women who have a history of sexual abuse) tend to have very unstable relationships and poor self-image, and to be very emotionally fragile and needy of reassurance and support. They are at high risk of self-harm and impulse behaviours.

Personality disorders can't be cured with medication, although antidepressants and anti-psychotic drugs can help people to manage distressing feelings and behaviours. Personality disorders respond best to talking treatments, such as cognitive behavioural therapy and group therapy. These are aimed at helping the person acknowledge the difficulties their attitudes and behaviours create (for themselves and other people), and to learn healthier and more appropriate ways of behaving and interacting with others.

Personality disorder is not an accepted diagnosis for children and young people aged under 18. They may be described instead as having patterns of behaviour similar to personality disorders.

Other mental disorders

Bipolar disorder

Bipolar disorder used to be called manic depression. Both terms describe the extreme mood swings (from one polar point to the polar opposite, or from mania to depression). The person's mood can swing from feeling omnipotent and on top of the world to deepest, suicidal depression.

Some people on a bipolar "high" become convinced they are very rich, or that they have super-powers. This can make them do strange and extreme things, including spending money they don't have. People on a high tend to talk quickly and are very energetic and seem to need hardly any sleep. They can also take risks and get angry and impatient if other people try to stop them.

Bipolar disorder is cyclical, so an extreme high is frequently followed by an extreme low, when the person is unable to work, can't cope with ordinary life or take care of themselves, and can see no point in living. People with bipolar disorder are at very great risk of suicide. Cycles tend to recur regularly, over weeks or months or years, and can also be triggered by stressful or adverse events.

Bipolar disorder is mostly treated with medication. People can also learn how to manage their bipolar disorder by looking out for signs that they are starting on an up or down cycle and taking medication to try to prevent it. They can be helped to identify triggers and warning signs so that they can change their lifestyle and avoid stressful situations.

Schizophrenia and psychosis

Psychosis is a collective term used to describe symptoms of severe mental disorder that can include hallucinations, delusions and thought disorder (disorganised and disconnected thought processes and speech).

Schizophrenia is a form of psychosis. The "positive" symptoms of schizophrenia include hallucinations (hearing voices and seeing, feeling or even smelling things that no one else can), delusions (believing things that aren't based on what is really happening), and disordered thinking. Sometimes people believe they are being controlled by outside forces, like the TV or radio, or electronic radio waves, or other people. Having a psychotic breakdown can be terrifying for the person – they may hear voices that tell them to harm themselves, or (more rarely) others.

People with schizophrenia can feel confused and unable to concentrate. They can also feel very low in energy and emotionally flat. They may feel unable to motivate themselves to do anything and can neglect their health, hygiene and appearance. These are known as "negative" symptoms. People with these symptoms can very easily become socially disengaged and isolated, and are likely to experience harassment and stigma because of their strange behaviours and neglected appearance.

Schizophrenia is mostly treated with anti-psychotic medication. Anti-psychotics are powerful tranquillisers. They are not a "cure" for schizophrenia, but they can help to reduce the effects of the symptoms, the hallucinations and delusions, so that the person feels less distressed and frightened. Some of the side effects of the medications are similar to the "negative" symptoms of schizophrenia, including drowsiness, muddled thinking, agitation and restlessness, and difficulty in talking. They can also cause weight gain and tremors, which are often mistaken for symptoms of the mental disorder itself.

CBT can help people with schizophrenia to understand and manage the symptoms of their disorder. CBT-based family therapy can help families who are living with and caring for someone with a severe mental disorder.

Schizophrenia tends to recur and can be a lifelong disorder. Special mental health services have been set up for young people when they first develop the symptoms. These "early intervention in psychosis" services are based on the theory that treating the symptoms quickly and at the same time addressing other aspects (family, school, college, employment, social networks, etc) of the young person's life will stop them from spiralling down into lifelong severe mental disorder and social exclusion. These early intervention services have been found to be more effective than routine mental health care, although that may be simply because the young person is receiving more intensive, age-appropriate psychosocial care that is genuinely aimed at keeping them in contact with, and helping them get back into, ordinary life.

Cannabis and psychosis
There is a growing awareness of the risk of cannabis-induced psychosis, particularly among young people. Studies show that a young person under the age of 15 who smokes cannabis is at four times greater risk of developing psychosis in early adulthood.

Some young people appear much more vulnerable to psychosis from even quite moderate use of cannabis; many others are unaffected. This may be due in part to the quality or strength of the cannabis, or to a genetic vulnerability in the young person.

For one in ten users, cannabis can result in short-term symptoms of psychosis, with hallucinations and delusionary thinking, but these tend to pass within a few days at most. There is also evidence of a link between smoking cannabis in adolescence and depression and anxiety in adulthood.

Other mental disorders in children

Eating disorders

Eating disorders are most common among girls and young women, but they also occur, and more often these days, among boys and young men. Eating disorders are often accompanied by compulsive exercising, particularly among boys and men.

Someone with anorexia will severely restrict their food and fluid intake, and may compulsively exercise, in order to control their weight. This can be very dangerous if the young person becomes severely malnourished. Someone with bulimia will alternate between binge-eating and self-induced vomiting. People with bulimia may not lose as much weight or as evidently, but the bouts of over-eating and vomiting can severely damage their health.

Eating disorders are commonly misunderstood as "slimmer's diseases". There is a widespread misunderstanding that young women develop eating disorders because they are trying to be fashionably thin. However, the causes of anorexia and bulimia are much more complex. They are associated with an array of family and individual factors, including low self-esteem, parental pressure, bullying, family breakdown, and childhood abuse and neglect.

SECTION I

Eating disorders can kill. If a young person becomes severely malnourished they may be very vulnerable to infections. Anorexia nervosa can also lead to lifelong osteoporosis (brittle bones). Eating disorders are hard to treat although some specialist therapeutic approaches, including family therapy for younger children, have been successful. Sometimes, if the weight loss becomes dangerous, the child will have to be admitted to hospital to be helped to regain a healthy body weight. However, these days it is generally agreed that children are much better treated in the community, and that the best approach is to try to help their families care for them, while tackling the individual difficulties that have triggered the eating disorder in the child.

Self-harm

Self-harm should not be confused with attempted suicide. Young people who repeatedly self-harm do not intend to end their life. Common forms of self-harm include cutting, burning, scalding, pulling out hair, hitting, and swallowing poisonous or caustic substances or taking overdoses of prescribed or over-the-counter medication. Often, adults regard self-harm as attention-seeking, but in many cases it will be hidden and will only come to light if the young person needs medical attention.

Young people who self-harm say they do this because it helps them deal with feelings of extreme unhappiness or anger; hurting themselves temporarily makes them feel better and provides a release for their emotions. Sometimes people find it easier to hurt themselves than to deal with whoever or whatever it is that is really hurting them.

Young people have described being treated unsympathetically by inexperienced or untrained casualty staff who do not understand what motivates self-harm. They say that trying to shame them or forcibly prevent them from self-harming does not help, because it is an important coping mechanism for them. In surveys, young people say it is more effective to help them find ways to harm themselves safely, so they don't cause serious damage, and try to help them deal with the problems in their lives that trigger the self-harm. Less damaging ways to self-harm include holding ice cubes or "pinging" an elastic band on the wrist.

Conduct disorders

The term "conduct disorder" in children describes a range of behaviours that are exaggerated and potentially harmful versions of normal child behaviours. They include persistent and repeated anti-social, aggressive and disruptive behaviour and excessive, unreasonable disregard for limits and boundaries. The child may become unmanageable and be unable to socialise or be taught with other children. One form of conduct disorder is oppositional defiant disorder (ODD), which basically means that the child persistently and repeatedly won't do as he (or she, but mostly he) is told, well beyond ordinary naughtiness or disobedience.

Conduct disorders have a number of causes, including poor parenting, difficulties at school, hyperactivity, lack of boundary setting, marital problems in the home, abuse, bereavement and other significant losses, and learning difficulties. There is a direct link between childhood conduct disorders and the possibility of developing mental disorder, personality disorder and criminality in adulthood.

The most effective treatments are individual and group parenting programmes for the parents or carers and behavioural and cognitive therapies for the children.

Hyperkinetic disorder/ADHD

There are a number of different terms used to describe the behaviours of children who are overactive and have difficulty concentrating. In the UK the terms commonly used are hyperkinetic disorder, attention deficit hyperactivity disorder

(ADHD) and hyperactivity. (The term Attention Deficit Disorder (ADD) is sometimes used in the US.)

The causes of hyperkinetic disorder are not fully understood. There is thought to be a strong genetic component. Hyperkinetic disorder is more common in boys than girls, although this may simply be because the diagnostic criteria are developed from studies of boys, and girls have different symptoms and manifestations.

Children with a hyperkinetic disorder can be very restless and fidgety. They may talk continuously and interrupt frequently. They can be easily distracted and find it hard to concentrate and complete tasks. They can be impulsive and oblivious to risk, and may struggle to wait their turn for attention. These are all normal '"symptoms" of childhood, of course. To have a formal diagnosis, the child must be showing these behaviours persistently and repeatedly over a long period of time.

These behaviours are common in most children. They only become a problem that may need treatment when they affect the child's social, family and school life, making it hard for him or her to learn and to make friends, and hard for the school and family to manage.

The condition can be treated with medication, but there is also some concern about giving young children powerful stimulant drugs at a time when their brains are still developing. Non-medical treatments include family therapy, individual child therapy, and alternative approaches such as changing the child's diet to exclude processed food and foods with high levels of artificial additives. The recommended treatment for severe hyperkinetic disorder is behavioural and/or family therapy in combination with medication. Less severe disorder should be treated with behavioural therapy, certainly in the first instance.

Hyperkinetic disorder can persist into adulthood and can continue to create problems for the individual because of the effects on their educational achievement and subsequent employment prospects, as well as their ability to cope with relationships and social situations.

Autistic spectrum disorders (ASD)

Autistic spectrum disorders affect around one in 100 children, and include autism and Asperger's syndrome. The common features of ASD are:

- difficulties with social interaction and communication;

- obsessive, ritualised behaviours; and

- obsessive collecting of facts and information and objects.

Some people (although ASD affects mostly boys and men) are affected only mildly and can cope with the demands of ordinary social life and relationships. Children with severe autism may find it almost impossible to communicate. They are likely to struggle to make friends and can find it very hard to learn in mainstream school if there are no extra resources to help teachers manage their particular behaviours and meet their learning needs.

Some symptoms of ASD can be managed by behavioural therapies. Medication may be prescribed to reduce the effects of very obsessive and compulsive behaviours. However, ASD cannot be "cured".

SECTION I

CHAPTER **4**

Who can help?

In the first instance, if your child is showing symptoms of mental health problems, you should go to your GP. Some GP practices employ counsellors who may be able to help children with depression and anxiety disorders. Your GP will be able to carry out an initial assessment and refer you to other sources of specialist help, including your local Child and Adolescent Mental Health Service (CAMHS), where you will have access to a range of mental health experts.

Mental health experts

A child psychiatrist is a medically trained doctor who specialises in treating children's mental health problems. They can prescribe medication, make referrals to a range of therapies and, in extreme cases, may admit the child to a specialist children's inpatient mental health unit for a while, especially if they think the child's physical health and wellbeing could be at risk due to their condition.

A clinical psychologist has had training at postgraduate level in how the mind works. They can conduct clinical assessments using a range of tools, such as psychological tests, interviews and direct observation of behaviour, to explore a child's difficulties. Based on these assessments, they can offer therapy (often with a cognitive behavioural focus), counselling and advice if they have completed further training in this field. They generally work in NHS child and adolescent mental health teams or social services, although some work in private practice.

A cognitive behavioural therapist can guide the child to find more helpful, less distressing ways of seeing the world and themselves and of interacting with other people. They can also teach techniques for managing obsessive thoughts or behaviours and getting out of negative patterns of thinking.

A family therapist works with the whole family to help them find ways to help each other when a child is experiencing emotional or behavioural difficulties. They mostly work with all the close family together, but they also see individual family members on their own. They often use cognitive behavioural techniques and draw on the resources of family members to find solutions to problems, individually and together. They work holistically, taking the family's circumstances into account. Their aim is to help the individual child change, but also to help the rest of the family change so that they can support the child's sustained recovery after the family therapy is ended.

A child psychotherapist offers psychoanalytic treatment to children and young people with emotional or behavioural difficulties. They use a range of approaches, including integrative arts, humanistic, transactional analysis and systemic

SECTION 1

psychotherapies (see www.bacp.co.uk for more information). They may see a child individually, in a group with other children, or with parents or other family members. They may also see parents or carers without the child being present. They tailor their approach to the individual child and work in an age-appropriate way – for example, they may use play with younger children. They will see infants and parents together so that their patterns of interaction can be observed.

Child mental health nurses have done special, additional training in child development and mental health problems in children. They work in children's mental health units, or in community-based children's services, often alongside social workers, family therapists and educational psychologists.

Consent to treatment and the Mental Health Act

The Mental Health Acts of 1983 and 2007 set out the legal framework for voluntary and compulsory hospital admission and treatment for children and young people.

- Young people aged 16–17 years can decide for themselves if they wish to go into a psychiatric hospital voluntarily, and their decision cannot be overruled by their parents.

- A child aged under 16 can give consent to treatment and hospital admission if they are deemed mentally competent to do so (that is, mentally capable of understanding the implications of the decision).

- If the child is aged under 16 and is deemed not able to give informed consent, their parents may be able to consent on their behalf, but only if the decision falls within what is called the "zone of parental control". The test for this is whether the decision is one that would normally be taken by a parent, and whether there are any concerns that they might not make a decision in the best interests of the child.

- If the child, young person or his or her parents refuse to consent to treatment or hospital admission, and the medical authorities feel it is in the child's best interests to be treated in hospital, they may need to invoke the Mental Health Act. The law on compulsory mental health treatment is highly complex and expert advice should be sought. "Rethink", the national mental health charity, has published a very helpful explanation of the processes (Rethink, 2008), which is also available to download from its website at www.rethink.org.

By law, a child or young person's parents will only be consulted and informed about their mental health and treatment if the child gives consent. Parents do not have an automatic right to be informed or consulted unless there are very strong reasons to override the child's refusal (i.e. the child might be at serious risk of harm).

Under the 2007 Mental Health Act, hospitals must ensure that children and young people are treated in age-appropriate settings. Children aged under 16 should never be admitted to an adult psychiatric ward, and young people aged 16–17 should only be admitted to adult psychiatric wards in exceptional circumstances. These are:

- in an emergency, when there is no alternative and then only as a short-term solution;

- in atypical circumstances when it is appropriate for the individual young person (i.e. if the young person is nearly 18 and is being treated by an Early Intervention Service with beds on an adult ward).

The Code of Practice attached to the Mental Health Act also spells out what should be provided on a hospital ward for children and young people. This includes:

- age-appropriate facilities;

- staff with specialist training, skills and knowledge to meet the mental health and psychosocial needs of children and young people;

- a hospital routine that ensures their personal, social and educational development can continue as normally as possible;

- the same access to educational opportunities as their peers outside hospital, if they are well enough to make use of them.

CHAPTER 5

Nature and nurture

Why do some children develop mental health problems and not others? The answer lies partly in nature, and partly in nurture, and wholly in the interaction between the two.

Risk factors

Some children are genetically at greater risk of developing mental health problems because they have inherited a gene, or set of genes in combination, that makes them more vulnerable to mental disorder when exposed to particular stressors or environmental factors.

The most important factor is the quality of parenting. Children whose parents have poor parenting skills are at greater risk of mental disorder. If a child does not have a secure attachment with his or her parent/primary caregiver, he or she is more at risk of mental health and conduct problems. So, too, are children whose parents use emotional punishment.

A major risk factor for mental disorder in childhood is physical, emotional and/or sexual abuse and neglect. The effects on the child are huge, and can be life-long.

There are other risk factors for mental health problems in children. If the mother smokes, takes drugs or drinks alcohol during pregnancy, her child is at greater risk of long-term neurological damage and emotional, learning and mental health problems. Stress during pregnancy and low birth weight may also be linked with mental health problems in childhood.

Children brought up in low-income families and in families where neither parent has educational qualifications are at higher risk of mental ill health. This is not to suggest that poorer families are worse at bringing up their children, but simply that the socio-economic difficulties associated with poverty and deprivation are also associated with a greater risk of mental disorders in children.

However, not all children exposed to the same kinds and levels of difficulties will develop mental health problems and not all will experience ill effects throughout their life. So which factors increase a child's risk of mental disorder, and which protect them?

Resilience

Resilience is the term commonly used in child mental health and development to describe what it is that protects a child when exposed to stressors that could lead to mental health problems. Resilience is both intrinsic to the child (i.e. part of the child's personality) and extrinsic (i.e. nurtured and reinforced by positive external factors).

A child's resilience to the stresses that can lead to mental health problems is determined by a combination of individual, family and community/environmental factors.

- At an individual level, research shows that children are more resilient to mental health problems if they are confident; believe in themselves and their abilities; feel in control of their lives and that they can sort out their problems or get help with any difficulties; are good at communicating and at making friends; can think ahead and plan; are thoughtful rather than impulsive; have a sense of humour, and have hobbies and interests.

- At a family level, children are more resilient to possible mental health problems and conduct disorders if they have a close and trusting relationship with at least one adult who is a consistent and positive presence in their life (it doesn't have to be a birth parent or even a family member); if they have close grandparents; if their family unit is stable and isn't fractured by frequent or major separations or losses, and if they have close siblings (but not too many of them – four or fewer). Money and material possessions also help.

- At a societal level, living in a friendly, community-minded neighbourhood, with lots of contact with children of their own age, attending a good school where they are happy and enjoy their education, and positive adult role models all help to boost a child's resilience.

Conversely, negative influences such as abuse and neglect, parental drug or alcohol misuse, parental mental health problems and living in poverty reduce a child's resilience to mental disorders.

Children with the highest levels of resilience appear to be

those who believe they can deal with, or resolve the problems in their life.

Heritability

Despite the continuing search for the "schizophrenia gene" and huge leaps forward in the identification of genes that are linked with specific mental health problems, there is little doubt that mental disorder is a product of the interaction between genes and the environment (nature and nurture).

Numerous controlled trials and studies have been conducted to compare and identify the independent influences of genetic inheritance and the child's family environment. These generally compare the long-term mental health outcomes of children adopted from birth with those of children raised in their birth families. Studies have also explored the influence of their family and social environment on a child's mental health and lifelong outcomes.

From this research, we know that a child with a history of mental disorder in their birth family, even if adopted from birth, is at greater risk of developing mental disorder than a child without mental disorder in their birth family. However, that risk is significantly increased where the same child is exposed to poor parenting, family breakdown and instability and socio-economic deprivation.

We also know that adopted children generally are at greater risk of mental disorders than children brought up in a caring birth family, because most of them have had difficult experiences in the important early years. So the heritability issue is far from clear-cut.

Statistically, the risk of a child of parents (one or both) with a severe mental disorder also developing the same disorder is quite high. One major population study has calculated the risk of a child developing schizophrenia at about one per cent if neither parent has the disorder, seven per cent if one parent has schizophrenia, and 28 per cent if both parents have the condition. For bipolar disorder, the risks are less than one per cent if neither parent has the disorder, five per cent if one parent does and 25 per cent if both parents do. There is a similar raised risk if one parent has schizophrenia and the other bipolar disorder (16 per cent risk of the child developing schizophrenia and 12 per cent risk of the child developing bipolar disorder). The risk of the child developing any psychiatric disorder if their parents both have schizophrenia is 68 per cent, and 45 per cent if they both have bipolar disorder. These statistics refer to children raised in their birth family (Gottesman et al, 2010).

Figure 1 shows the estimated heritability of the nine most prevalent mental disorders (Uher and McGuffin, 2008). Autism, schizophrenia and bipolar disorder carry the highest genetic risk for children.

However, there is equally strong evidence of the influence of the child's upbringing and the interaction of genetic predisposition with the child's environment. For example, poverty may "trump" heritability: the adopted child of parents with no mental disorder is at greater risk of developing psychosis if he or she is raised in a family living on low income and in a deprived area (Wicks et al, 2010). Furthermore, genetic heritability may predispose a child towards mental disorder if they do not receive adequate parenting: there is evidence that adopted children of birth parents with a mental disorder are more sensitive to the negative effects of poor parenting in their adoptive families (Tienari et al, 2004).

Figure 1: Estimated heritability of mental disorders

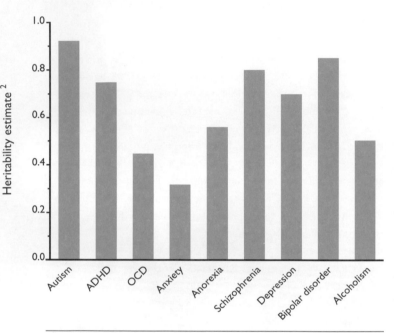

(Reproduced from *Genetics of Mental Ill Health in Children and Adults and Interaction of Genes with Social Factors*, Uher and McGuffin, 2008, © Crown copyright. This information is licensed under the terms of the Open Government Licence)

A particularly important study (Gonzales-Pinto *et al*, 2011) has found that being brought up in an abusive family environment increases the child's risk of severe mental disorder, regardless of family history. The same study also produced clear and encouraging evidence that being brought up in a positive family environment protects against mental disorder, regardless of genetic risk.

---

[2] The heritability estimate reflects the proportion of variability allocated to additive genetic effect.

Another study (Wynne *et al*, 2006) has found that, while high genetic risk and poor parenting are highly predictive of a child developing schizophrenia, low genetic risk or positive parenting can be protective.

The current prevailing expert view appears to be that heritability alone does not explain mental disorder; nor, on their own, do the child's upbringing and family socio-economic circumstances.

Put very simply, negative factors such as abuse and neglect have a significant impact on the child's developing "social brain" if they occur during sensitive periods in his or her development, and this renders them more vulnerable to an existing propensity to mental disorder (van Os *et al*, 2010). It would be completely wrong to believe that any child with a family history of severe mental disorder is doomed to have mental health problems themselves. Even children with a very high genetic risk can avoid developing severe mental disorder if raised in a positive family environment. But this is subject to many variables (both in the child and the adoptive family). It would be equally wrong for adoptive parents to blame themselves if their child does develop severe mental disorder, when so much damage may already have occurred pre-birth and in the first few months of the child's life.

SECTION I

CHAPTER 6

Family upbringing

If genes alone are not the cause of childhood mental disorder, what are the factors in a child's upbringing that place them at higher risk of developing mental health problems, regardless of, or in combination with, their genetic loading?

Understanding these issues may help to explain the difficult behaviours of an adopted child, however well he or she is parented in their adoptive family, and how their behaviours can be managed and the impact of their genetic inheritance lessened. Knowing where behaviours are coming from, and the difficulties with which the child is struggling, can also be reassuring for adoptive parents who may think they, or even their child, are "doing it wrong".

Science and the study of child development are building a very complex picture of the interlocked physiological and psychological processes that lay down the foundations for a child's lifelong mental and physical health and wellbeing. Increasingly, the evidence tells us that the roots of our mental and physical health lie in the womb and in our very early years.

Pregnancy and birth

Very low birth weight is linked with cognitive and behavioural problems in children, both in early childhood and later in life, with a greater risk of severe and common mental health problems in adulthood. Impaired cognitive ability is inevitably linked with poor educational outcomes.

If the mother smokes during pregnancy, drinks too much alcohol or takes certain drugs, this can lead to a range of problems in the child, including low birth weight. But it can also affect the child's long-term neurological and cognitive-emotional development, leading to lower intelligence, hyperkinetic disorders, conduct problems and poorer educational attainment. Maternal stress during pregnancy can similarly have a negative impact on the developing brain of the foetus, as well as leading to pre-term delivery and the associated ills of delayed physical and mental development.

Maternal mental disorder can affect the foetus and newborn infant. This is probably linked with the high levels of stress associated with mental ill health. Babies born to women who suffer from depression and anxiety during pregnancy are at higher risk of low birth weight. Mothers who have schizophrenia or bipolar disorder are at greater risk of pre-term delivery and having low birth weight infants, and their children are at higher risk of developmental delay.

Some scientists argue that apparent genetic predisposition to mental disorder in the children of mothers with mental disorder may be more about the effects of high levels of maternal stress while the child is still in the womb (see below on the effects of stress).

Attachment and the early years

To understand why the family environment and the child's upbringing in their very early years can lead to mental health problems, it is important to know a bit about child development theory, and attachment theory in particular.

Child psychiatrist and psychoanalyst John Bowlby originally developed the theory of attachment. Attachment describes the biological instinct of the human child to seek out their primary caregiver for comfort and reassurance when exposed to stressful situations, discomfort or pain. How the caregiver responds to the infant sets the pattern for the child's internal image of himself or herself and their parent, and their expectations of how other people will behave towards them. A frightened child who receives reassurance from his or her primary caregiver will have their expectation of comfort and safety confirmed. A child who is rebuffed, or even abused by their primary caregiver will feel confused and rejected and not know where to go for reassurance.

Bowlby's colleague Mary Ainsworth researched the theory with young children and their mothers, using what is known as the "Strange Situation" test. The child and mother are left alone in a playroom, under observation. A stranger then enters the room, and the parent leaves. The stranger tries to comfort the baby. The mother returns and comforts the child and the stranger leaves. The mother then goes out again and the stranger returns and once more tries to engage with the child. The mother finally comes back to comfort and play with her child.

How the child reacts to these experiences will depend on how "secure" their attachment is to their parent. Table 1 below describes the typical behaviour of children depending on their attachment style. Ainsworth identified three attachment styles: secure, insecure avoidant and insecure resistant. A fourth style, disorganised/disoriented, was added subsequently. Abused children tend overwhelmingly to belong to this fourth group. Table 1 describes the different behaviours typically shown by children in the four groups.

Table 1: Attachment styles in relation to behaviours in the Strange Situation test

Attachment style	Percentage of children at age one	Response in the Strange Situation
Secure	60–70 per cent	The child explores room with mother and is upset when she leaves. The child greets her happily when she returns and seeks her physical comfort.
Insecure avoidant	15–20 per cent	The child ignores mother and is not very distressed when she leaves the room. The child turns away from the mother when she returns.
Insecure resistant	10–15 per cent	The child explores the room with its mother but is anxious and stays close to her. The child is very distressed when the mother leaves and is ambivalent or angry when she returns and rejects physical comfort.
Disorganised/ disoriented	5–10 per cent	The child is very distressed when the mother leaves the room. On her return the child appears confused and unsure whether to approach or stay away from her.

Table 2 shows how these attachment styles may manifest in the child's behaviour, learning and social relationships at primary and secondary school age. (This table uses the term "avoidant" instead of "insecure avoidant", and "ambivalent" instead of "insecure resistant".)

Table 2: Attachment and learning styles across the school years

Stage	Secure	Avoidant	Ambivalent	Disorganised/ disoriented
Pre-school	Free to explore, think and feel	Explore, play flatly in a restricted or limited way and can be defensive in learning	Anxious diversion, attention-seeking, coercive and poor relating with peers	Fearful, disoriented, externalising and internalising
Primary	Success with peers and reading, coherent, good play and learning skills	Not fully connecting with peers, or exploring ideas and feelings	Attention seeking, self perceived as a victim and externalising	Language deficits/ impairments, poor metacognition, aggressive
Secondary	Coherent, popular and attuned to others	False sense of self and of others, defensive in errors and rejecting	Enmeshed in relationship problems, distracted, confused and uncertain	Academic failure, anxiety, criminal activity, negative thinking, incoherent and helpless

(Reproduced from Grieg et al, 2008. © Association of Educational Psychologists Nonproliferation Studies. Reprinted by permission of Taylor & Francis Ltd (www. tandfonline.com) on behalf of Association of Educational Psychologists)

Securely attached children are more curious, better able to cope with short-term stress and separation and more socialised than their insecurely attached peers. They are also better at "mentalising" – that is, they have a better understanding of their own thoughts and feelings and those of others, and have a better developed social understanding, which they have learned from their interactions with their mother/primary caregiver. They have, in child development terms, built up a secure "working model" of self and others.

This secure working model of themselves and of the reliability of others is thought to be crucial for a child's cognitive and social abilities throughout life. Insecurely attached children may be at greater risk of poor educational achievement, attention problems and language delay and impairment, with consequences for their educational and employment prospects in adult life. Securely attached children tend to have higher self-esteem, greater motivation to learn, better social skills and relationships, and consequently better lifetime outcomes (Grieg *et al*, 2008).

However, longitudinal studies (studies that follow up their subjects over many years) have found little or no continuity between childhood attachment patterns and attachment patterns in adulthood. Other factors (for example, poverty, adverse events or peer relations) may be equally, if not more important. Some children with mental disorders may be very securely attached. So, while the theory is extremely useful for understanding children's emotional behaviour patterns, it should not be seen as setting in stone how a child will relate to other people throughout life.

Moreover, there is evidence that foster carers who have received specialist training in caring for children from abusive homes can help to change a child's attachment patterns and that these children are able to develop trusting relationships with their foster or adoptive carers (Dozier *et al*, 2009).

Parental mental disorder

Children in families where there is mental disorder have been found to have poorer attachment and less well developed coping capacity than other children.

Parents who have a mental disorder may struggle to provide the sensitive, nurturing environment that is vital to healthy child development. This is by no means always the case, and may also depend on the nature of the mental disorder and how its symptoms manifest. But the symptoms of many mental disorders can affect a caregiver's ability to relate to others, including their child(ren).

The child of parents with schizophrenia may be exposed to both the symptoms of the parent's disorder (such as paranoia and delusions, erratic and unpredictable behaviours, low energy and low motivation) and lack of parental warmth, responsiveness, sensitivity and attention to their needs.

Depression can prevent a parent responding sensitively and appropriately to his or her child's needs for interaction and reassurance. Studies of the children of depressed mothers have found delayed language development and cognition, as well as conduct disorders, depression, poor social skills, sleeping problems, physical ill health and poor attachment. Maternal depression in the first three months of a child's life is linked with poor cognitive ability in the child and problems with concentration and learning at 11 years. Post-natal depression is also linked with behavioural problems in children, and with learning and socialisation difficulties in school at age five – particularly among boys. It has been estimated that up to 40 per cent of children of depressed parents have behaviour problems, placing them at between two and five times greater risk than other children. These children are also at greater risk of phobias and alcohol dependence.

If a child's primary carer is unable to recognise their child's needs because of their mental disorder or personality disorder, this can result in neglect or in inappropriate, intrusive and harmful interactions. Interestingly, children of parents with bipolar disorder appear less at risk of developmental harm.

Looked after children

Studies of looked after children demonstrate the negative effects of poor parenting, emotional deprivation, neglect and abuse on a child's long-term mental health and wellbeing.

A national survey of the mental health of looked after children and young people aged 5–17 years (Meltzer et al, 2002) found very high levels of mental disorder. Nearly half (45 per cent) had a mental disorder: 37 per cent had conduct disorders, 12 per cent had emotional disorders such as anxiety and depression, and seven per cent had a hyperkinetic disorder (some of these children may have had more than one disorder). However, the survey did not make any adjustment to these rates to allow for age at entry to local authority care or length of time in care. So we cannot tell from these statistics whether the rates of mental disorder were greater for those who had been in care the longest or came into care at a younger or older age.

The increased risks of mental ill health applied across all age groups.

- The 5–10-year-olds were five times more likely than children not in care to have a mental disorder (42 per cent compared with eight per cent). Of these, 11 per cent had emotional disorders, compared with three per cent in the general population. Thirty-six per cent had conduct disorders, compared with five per cent in the general population, and 11 per cent had hyperkinetic disorders, compared with two per cent in the general population.

- The 11–15-year-olds were four to five times more likely than children not in care to have a mental disorder – 12 per cent had emotional disorders, compared with six per cent in the general population. Forty per cent had conduct disorders, compared with six per cent in the general population, and seven per cent had kinetic disorders, compared with one per cent in the general population.

Conduct disorders were the most common mental health problem in looked after children.

The same survey compared outcomes for children in different kinds of placements. Children who remained in institutional residential care had the highest levels of mental disorder: 66 per cent compared with 40 per cent of children in foster care and children returned to their birth parents.

There was also a difference in the type of mental disorder. Children living with their birth parents or in residential care were twice as likely as those in foster care to have emotional disorders. Children living in residential care were much more likely than those in foster care or living with their birth parents to have conduct disorders (56 per cent vs 33 per cent and 28 per cent respectively).

Interestingly, this research found no links between the quality of the child's care before entry into the looked after system and their levels of mental disorder, nor with the reasons they came into care; being in residential care or being placed outside their home area was more likely to affect their mental health. Children with special educational needs and those who were excluded from school were also more likely to have higher mental health needs. Those with better mental health were less likely to have experienced several changes of placement.

Other research shows there is a clear link between the age of the child when he or she is taken into care, and the risk of mental disorders. The younger the child (and in consequence the less exposure they have had to poor or abusive parenting and harm), the less likely they are to have severe and ongoing mental disorders in later life (Tarren-Sweeney, 2008).

Adopted children

Adopted children have a similar level of emotional and behavioural problems to looked after children, even when successfully placed with adoptive families from a relatively young age. But the later the child is adopted, the greater the risk of problems: older children will have been exposed to greater risk of abuse and neglect over a longer period, and to have suffered the effects of being in care and the lack of a consistent, positive relationship with parents or caregivers.

One comparative study (Keyes et al, 2008) of adolescent children in the United States, who had been placed with their adoptive family before the age of two, found twice the risk of ADHD and oppositional defiant disorder (ODD) but, interestingly, no greater risk of conduct disorder, major depression or separation anxiety disorder. In fact, while the levels of ADHD and ODD in the adopted children affected were clinically very significant, overall the researchers concluded that most adopted children are psychologically very well adjusted. Importantly, they also collected evidence to show that the emotional and behavioural problems found in these adopted children were caused by their pre-adoption experiences, not by the fact of adoption itself.

Another study (Howard *et al*, 2004) compared the emotional and mental health of children adopted through different processes. This study found much higher levels of emotional and behavioural problems in children adopted from child welfare agencies than in children raised in their birth families, prior to adoption, or in children adopted from overseas and children adopted directly from birth (so-called domestic infant adoptions). A quarter of the children adopted via welfare agencies were rated by their parents as having emotional and mental health problems, compared with 14 per cent of domestic infant adoptions and six per cent of non-adopted children.

However, the finding that 41 per cent of adopted children were seeing a child counsellor or psychologist, compared with 18 per cent of the non-adopted children, could indicate a higher level of anxiety and/or willingness to seek help by the parents of adopted children. It was also interesting that 31 per cent of children adopted from welfare agencies and 30 per cent of domestic infant adoptions in this study were taking medication prescribed for behavioural problems, compared with just four per cent of non-adopted children. Again, did this suggest a greater readiness among parents and professionals to medicalise problems, or was it a straightforward reflection of greater clinical need?

Conclusion

Statistics can be made to show a multitude of things, but the conclusions we can take from these studies are laid out here.

- Taken together, these findings confirm the negative effects of a lack of a consistent, secure and loving family environment and of childhood abuse and neglect.

- They also point to the importance of secure

attachments for children's mental health and wellbeing, and the overall benefits of adoption for children.

- Studies that compare outcomes and the mental health of children who remain in institutional care with those of adopted and fostered children show overwhelmingly better results for the latter.

- The key factor in the better outcomes for foster and adopted children is the long-term consistent caring bonds they are able to develop with their adoptive parents/caregivers.

The next chapter explains in a simplified way the physiological processes that may place children at greater risk of developing emotional and behavioural problems, and the extent of the challenge facing adoptive parents and foster carers.

SECTION 1

CHAPTER 7

The neurobiology of child mental disorders and stress

We know that the lack of a warm, positive relationship with their primary caregiver and insecure attachment are strongly linked with subsequent behavioural and emotional problems in the child.

It may be helpful to understand the physiological processes that can explain why a child expresses the effects of abusive or traumatic experiences through mental health or behavioural disorders.

Neurobiologists have been researching what might be happening in a child's brain to drive these behaviours, with a particular emphasis on the physiological effects of stress. This research is still in its infancy and much is conjecture, for obvious reasons – it is impossible to know for certain what is happening inside a living child's brain. Much of the current theory is built on experimentation with animals. [3]

---

[3] This chapter draws on Glaser D (2000) 'Child abuse and neglect and the brain: a review', *Journal of Child Psychology & Psychiatry*, 41:1, pp 97–116.

The child's brain

A child's brain is very sensitive and very plastic (malleable), particularly in the first two years of life, when it undergoes a massive amount of development in a very short period of time. In normal, healthy child-rearing, the parents/caregiver will have a huge amount of interaction with the child. This interaction, often called "serve and return", stimulates the brain to form the synaptic connections in the frontal lobe that become the framework for the child's lifelong cognitive capacity and behaviour. The child does something, and the parent responds, and vice versa, as in a tennis game. These interactions should be sensitive, nurturing and predictable; the child should be protected from fear and stress, and from too much sensory input, and gently encouraged and supported to explore new things. If the child is secure in the knowledge that their parent is there to provide comfort, safety and reassurance, then the child will be securely attached.

Neglected and abused children do not have these kinds of interactions with their parent. Nor do they have the security of a safe base from which to explore the world and new experiences. This means the synaptic connections in their brain are not stimulated, which means the cognitive framework is not built. Parts of the brain may even die off, leaving (famously in the case of abandoned children found in Romania's orphanages after the fall of Ceausescu in 1989) a "black hole" in the frontal lobe – the part of the brain concerned with emotions, behaviour and cognition.

The frontal lobe is more highly developed in humans than in other mammals. This is the part of the brain that gives us the capacity to think ahead, to be aware of consequences of our actions, to build relationships with other people and to feel kindness, empathy and concern. It enables us to be self-aware, to solve problems, to be creative and to use our imagination. It also helps us to regulate our own emotions so that we can calm ourselves when we feel stressed.

These functions don't develop until the end of the first year of a child's life. A child who does not have a nurturing relationship with their parent does not learn how to express their emotions or how to regulate their stress levels by themselves.

When the role of this part of the brain and its importance in early childhood development are understood, it is easier to see why some adopted children from abusive families or families with a history of mental disorder or substance misuse behave as they do, and can struggle throughout life, despite a subsequent nurturing upbringing.

The brain of a child who is neglected, abused and/or under-stimulated in these early years will remain under-developed, leaving the child less able to learn and less likely to achieve their full potential and develop good social skills. It can also mean they behave in unusual and often anti-social ways, because those parts of their brain that govern social behaviours and emotions are under-developed, or simply not there.

Neurobiologists theorise that an abused, mistreated child will not be able to regulate their emotional responses to stressful situations. Their brain will not have the capacity to do so, resulting in inappropriate and difficult behaviours and, ultimately, mental disorders. The longer the child is exposed to abusive or neglectful parenting, the more difficult it will be to recover the lost connections in their brain. The child may be taught in later life, using cognitive behavioural techniques, how to behave and respond in certain situations, but they will lack the seemingly automatic and instinctive response of the child brought up in a safe and nurturing environment.

Stress

Neurobiologists are also making important discoveries about the physiological mechanisms of the human stress response system.

A small amount of stress is a good thing: it is a normal human response to the new, the unfamiliar and the unexpected. It heightens our senses. At its most basic, it enables us to "fight or flee" threat or danger. But when the stress is repeated, persistent and long term, without relief, it becomes literally toxic, and can lead to damage to parts of the brain, as well as major physical and mental health problems (including high risk of coronary heart disease and mental ill health such as depression) in adult life.

The stress response is the body's way of coping with frightening, unexpected and abusive situations. It is highly complex. Put very simply, it involves the hypothalamic-pituitary-adrenal (HPA) axis – the pathway connecting the brain to the adrenal cortex, which secretes the stress hormone cortisol into the blood stream. When cortisol is produced in response to exposure to stressful or frightening situations, it suppresses the body's immune response, increases the levels of glucose in the blood stream and dampens the fear response. These all improve the body's ability to deal with the threat.

This system is self-regulating, in that when certain parts of the brain register that the amount of cortisol in the blood stream has risen, they send a message via the HPA axis to the adrenal cortex to reduce the levels, so the body is not flooded with damaging amounts of cortisol and can return to homeostasis (this would be like taking the foot off the accelerator in a stationary car, so the engine returns to normal, idling state). If increased levels of cortisol are still needed (for example, in situations of extreme danger, requiring extra energy and strength), this too can be communicated via the HPA axis. Cortisol levels normally fluctuate over the course of the day – they are higher in the morning and reduce in the afternoon.

Another response to stress is certain kinds of behaviour. Interestingly, cortisol levels and these behaviours do not necessarily coincide. At age two to six months a child's raised cortisol levels and crying in response to fear or pain will be about equal. But in a healthy child at 15 months, crying will exceed the levels of cortisol. Studies have also found that giving a child a dummy will stop the crying behaviour, but the levels of cortisol will remain unaffected – the equivalent to the body's engine continuing to accelerate hard, even though the car is not moving.

Raised cortisol levels can be harmful to brain development. In particular, they affect the hippocampus. This is the part of the brain concerned with verbal and visual memory. High exposure to cortisol leads to hippocampal cell death.

Studies both of humans and animals show that reassuring, nurturing contact with the mother restores levels of cortisol to normal levels. Specifically, studies show that insecurely attached children are much more likely than securely attached children to have high levels of cortisol in their system when exposed to frightening situations. Children with a disorganised/disoriented attachment style are particularly vulnerable to raised cortisol levels when exposed to situations that securely attached children find only slightly scary.

Long-term exposure to stress has been found to lead to passive and withdrawn behaviour ("learned hopelessness"), which neurobiologists explain as the body's attempt to control the flood of cortisol within normal, manageable limits.

Another important part of the body's stress response system is the adrenal gland. This secretes adrenaline and noradrenaline, which increase the heart rate and blood pressure, cause sweating, and activate the body's "fight or flight" response to stress. Persistent and repeated raised levels of these hormones may be linked to the impulsive behaviour and short attention span associated with ADHD.

The difficult behaviours of abused children can thus be described in terms of the body's physiological responses to extended and repeated stress, and the excess release of adrenaline and cortisol.

Research suggests that exposure to adverse environments and abuse has a greater effect than genetic vulnerability or resilience.

The good news is that early intervention to remove the child from the source of stress and provide safety and reassurance can prevent long-term damage to his or her mental health and wellbeing. In studies of rats, the hippocampal cell death caused in the brains of young rats by the stress of being removed for a prolonged period from their mother is reversed by her vigorous licking when they are returned to her. This mirrors the effects of the focused, highly nurturing care described in the previous chapter on attachment theory, which has been shown to restore a child's ability to develop secure attachment patterns and trusting relationships (Dozier et al, 2009).

SECTION I

Conclusion

Much of this book is necessarily gloomy, concerned as it is with the bad things that can happen when a child comes into this world with a legacy of mental ill health in the family and/or is exposed to abuse and maltreatment in their very early years. The harsh truth is that damage in the womb, genetic vulnerability and abuse and neglect in a child's early years can (on their own and in toxic combination) permanently harm a child and blight their life.

However, as demonstrated by the testimonies that follow from parents who have adopted children from deprived and abusive backgrounds, or with a high genetic loading for mental disorder, it is possible to make a very big difference – mostly by doing nothing more sophisticated than offering unconditional love, stability, constancy and security. But it needs to be acknowledged that this can be difficult with some children, who may have very challenging behaviour.

Below are some recommendations for adoptive parents provided by Professor Stephen Scott, Consultant Child and Adolescent Psychiatrist, and Professor of Child Health and Behaviour at the Institute of Psychiatry, who heads the National Specialist Conduct Problems Clinic and the National Specialist Adoption and Fostering Clinic, and is Director of Research at the National Academy for Parenting Practitioners.

- Always try to be warm, not cold and withdrawn, despite provocation.

- Be firm and follow through with calm strategies. Don't indulge the child because you think they have had a hard past. Don't be hostile and critical either – children who were abused are far more sensitive to hostile tones and it can set off their stress hormones much more readily than is the case with other children.

- Have explanations in your head that help you stay calm and respond strategically and remind you that the child's behaviours are not personal to you or an intentional attack on you. Tell yourself, 'It's his ADHD' or 'She can't help it, she can't regulate her feelings', or whatever seems appropriate and helpful for you.

- Do ask for help from a Child and Adolescent Mental Health team. If you aren't happy with their response and the care and treatment they offer, ask for a second opinion. These teams are highly trained experts in child and adolescent mental health issues, and should be able to offer skilled assessment, referral and treatment, as well as advice on the day-to-day management of problems.

PARENTING CHILDREN AFFECTED BY MENTAL HEALTH PROBLEMS

JEANNIE AND GORDON; ELLEN AND BOB, JENNY AND DANIEL; ANGELA AND DAVID, CHARLOTTE AND JACK; AND ABBY AND JIM, HARRY AND APRIL.

Jeannie and Gordon

Gordon was 10 when he came to live with Jeannie Mackenzie. He'd previously been in local authority care. Jeannie was in her early 30s. She was unmarried, a qualified teacher who had worked with emotionally disturbed children in a residential school, so she knew what the difficulties might be if she adopted an older child. She didn't feel she could adopt a baby, but she wanted to offer an older child a home.

Jeannie's story

Immediately I heard about Gordon I felt he was someone I could offer a home to. We met twice, and he had one overnight stay and I said, 'This is hard on both of us', so the next weekend I fetched him home for good.

You foster the child initially for six months before you

apply for adoption but I was always very clear in my mind that I was going to adopt him. I didn't think it was right to say, 'Let's see how it goes'. That's setting you both up for failure. But it was tremendously risky, the whole process. I knew very little about him, and I wasn't told as much as I might have been – I don't know whether that was because social services didn't know either. I was told he had temper tantrums and that he had been in a psychiatric unit because of suicide risk; it was felt he would be safer there. But in fact, when I went to pick him up, I discovered he was on a locked ward, and clearly he was sedated.

He had no diagnosis. I was told his father had been violent towards him and his siblings, and that's what his birth mother told me later when I made contact with her. From her I learned his father had a mental disorder that was undiagnosed and untreated, that he was very volatile and irrational and would have uncontrollable violent episodes and that Gordon's paternal grandfather was the same. There was a lot of drinking as far as his father was concerned.

In fact, Gordon didn't have temper tantrums, as Jeannie discovered: they were early symptoms of what would later be diagnosed as bipolar disorder.

For several months he didn't have any attacks and I thought, whatever it was, it would be OK now he was in a settled environment. I had this very optimistic view of things.

When it first happened it was quite a shock. He became like another person, quite violent and aggressive but only ever towards himself and his possessions, not other people. The most disturbing and upsetting thing was you didn't feel he was emotionally present during these attacks. You couldn't talk to him, he wouldn't respond to you. He would be responding to someone else.

The rest of the time things went very well. He was very clear this was his home, I was his mum and this was where he wanted to be. That gave me the motivation to get it right.

She didn't seek help from social services or psychiatrists.

I was afraid that if I admitted I was struggling he might be taken away or put back into the psychiatric unit and, whatever happened, I didn't want him to go back into care. He was very happy to be in a normal environment and have a normal home.

I was worried that if I said I was concerned, his problems might have been medicalised and he would have been drugged – there would have been too much involvement of professionals. The school wanted me to refer him to the educational psychologist. I had a good relationship with the school because I am a teacher myself, so I asked them what we'd gain from it. I said he'd had a lot of psychological interventions in the past and I didn't want to put him through that again unless there was something to be gained and they weren't clear what they thought would be gained, so we didn't refer him.

Jeannie thinks that sometimes people seek a professional or medical solution too quickly; that we have lost trust in our own human capacity to help each other and find our own solutions.

I think we often go too quickly for the professional solution, the medical solution, the chemical solution, when we have what is needed within ourselves. Maybe other parents in my situation would have wanted more "expert" support. You need to find the solution that suits you and works best for you. Sometimes what you need is to talk to your own family and friends. It's often better if people talk to each other.

What people with mental disorder need are security and consistency and respect and the support of family and friends. For me, that comes first.

I had enormous back up from my family and friends, and from neighbours and colleagues. I was working at Barnardo's at the time so colleagues knew about children's behaviours and weren't fazed. But the couple living next door had no experience of that, and yet they were very understanding. They saw Gordon turn the house upside down and trash it and they came in and helped me set it straight and had no problem with him. They weren't afraid. Other people would take him for a while to give me a break.

He had these episodes less with other people, which worried me at first but then I realised it was because he felt safe with me, secure enough to show his worst side. As he grew up and could reflect on his behaviour better, he said he could keep a lid on things, manage things outside the home – that he'd be holding on all day at school and then, when he came home, whoosh!

He would bang his head and destroy things that were important to him. He made one or two suicide attempts that weren't lethal but they were an indicator of the level of distress he was feeling. He overdosed and he cut himself. Then I did go to the GP.

Fairly early on I thought, this is not "acting out". I had seen acting out and this was not it. I thought, there's something going on in his mind that isn't working, so what are the triggers and how can we manage it, and – just as important – how can he manage it?

One of the things that seemed to work well was being outdoors. It's the same now he's 37. He learned to identify when he was building up to an episode and to say, 'I need to go out'.

We created charts together with lists of what he could do when he felt things were building up. I learned very quickly not to try to contain him, not to interfere too much, and to reduce anything stressful around him. Some male friends would try telling him to stop it – they thought I wasn't being tough enough. But he'd be much better when he could get out of the house and go for a walk. I also tried diet – particularly in the early days. Additives didn't affect him but increasing vitamins, vitamin B complex – that seemed to help.

There was just one time when Jeannie felt she really was at the end of her tether and felt she couldn't go to her friends or family for help. Then she did call social services.

There was one night when he was about 12 when things were very bad. Usually I would phone a friend and ask them to come around but that night I didn't want to, so I phoned the emergency social work team and they said someone would come out.

SECTION II

In the half hour it took them to come I changed my mind, but I was very fortunate: the social worker came in, listened to what I said and asked if she could speak to Gordon. She talked to him and asked him what he wanted, and he said, 'Don't take me away'. I wasn't even thinking that I would ask for him to be taken away. But she handled it extremely well. She spent about an hour with us and then she asked, 'Do you feel you can go on?' and I said 'Yes'.

I was really saying, 'Help, I can't do it at the moment'. It was such a relief to be able to tell the social worker my worst feelings that I wouldn't want my friends and family to know. That night I felt suicidal; I couldn't see any way out, and I couldn't say that to family and friends. I didn't want to abandon Gordon.

Gordon wasn't formally referred for treatment until he was in his late teens, when he finally told Jeannie he was hearing malignant voices.

As he got older, the upsets got a lot worse – he had all that and then puberty kicked in as well. Then, when he was 17 or 18, he had a very different upset. He was working at a local farm – he had a job there – and he came home saying he wasn't very well. He was shaking. He lay down and curled into a foetal position. I asked what was wrong and he said, 'I can't manage any more with the voices'. That was the first time he had said to me he was hearing voices telling him what to do. He'd been hearing voices for a long time but hadn't wanted to tell anyone.

I contacted his doctor who wanted to admit him to hospital but Gordon didn't want to go. He agreed to take the medication and we saw a psychiatric nurse, but Gordon didn't like him at all.

I am not sure it would have made any difference if I had known about the episodes when I adopted him, or if I would have reacted differently. I still think I was right not to have him labelled or risk him being sent to a special educational facility. He managed in mainstream schools despite his difficulties.

When Gordon was 18 he met a Canadian woman and decided he wanted to marry her. They moved to Canada. When he had another psychotic episode, he was referred to a psychiatrist and diagnosed with bipolar disorder.

He said it was the first time he'd talked to someone who understood what it was like and made sense to him. He's been seeing the same psychiatrist now for 15 years, and he's only been in hospital twice. He manages his condition very well. He is very determined and positive and will do his utmost to make it work.

Jeannie also got married, when Gordon was 27 and had long left home – to someone who also had adopted children. She and her husband share three children and five grandchildren, including Gordon's son and daughter. Gordon told her husband, 'I want you to be my dad'.

Jeannie hopes their experiences will be helpful to others. Her advice to adoptive parents is:

- Have confidence in your own abilities and capacities to help your child.

  For me, I think the important message for other adoptive parents is to be aware of how much you have to offer. I'm not saying don't involve professionals, but be aware that what professionals can offer is limited. What's important is finding from within yourself what you have to support the child.

- Don't automatically seek medical solutions to emotional/behavioural problems.

  Nobody knows your child like you do. Other people can offer advice and support but they are not living with the situation on a daily basis. Sometimes the advice isn't practical and you think, 'Get real!' You are with the child 24/7. The professionals can't care as much as you care. It's about finding that inner strength and confidence that you know your child best and care enough to try to find a solution.

- Don't think you can manage it alone – talk to and involve your family and friends.

  Talking to people, to friends and family, is really important. I always had a great need to talk about what was happening; I couldn't have coped without being able to talk.

  Your GP can be very helpful. I talked to the GP about Gordon's terrible sleeping problems and he understood that I didn't want to put him on medication. He reassured me that what I was doing – giving him camomile tea and encouraging him to go for walks

to tire himself out – would be fine. He just said, 'Go
ahead, try it'.

- Work with the school – be honest with them about the
  challenges and tell them how they can help you.

  It helped that, having worked in schools, I talked their
  language. Be open with the teachers, involve them,
  explain the situation and why your child behaves this
  way. Be willing to share what works with them, if they
  are willing to listen. The teaching staff would ask me
  what to do. I told them, 'If you see it building up, in his
  body language, tell him to go out and walk around the
  playground for a couple of minutes'.

Gordon's story

*Gordon now lives permanently in Canada, although he
comes to the UK whenever he can to see Jeannie. He
has managed to keep well, apart from two hospital
admissions, and sees his psychiatrist regularly. He is still
much happier outdoors, and earns his living as a farm
worker in the winter and a beekeeper's assistant in the
summer.*

Working with bees is good for me, I have to slow
down. With bees, the whole thing is to be calm, slow,
methodical. Bees sense fear and as soon as they smell it,
you're done.

*Looking back on his childhood with Jeannie, Gordon
says that what made all the difference was that she
was always there for him and never lied to him.*

SECTION II

Persistence. I could see, I am sure, many a time she was thinking, 'What is the little bugger doing now?' But she was constant, steady: 'I am here, I am not leaving, I am not leaving.' Because that was something I desperately needed to know. So often people had said that to me and then whoosh, the rug under my feet was gone.

It was nothing fancy-dancy – it was just, 'I am here, you can tell me whatever and I won't think any less of you.'

I know she probably got criticised but she gave me a long enough leash that I could just go off on long walks. She was willing to rely on the fact that I liked being home, I liked having hugs, I liked my bedroom and I didn't want to run away.

I'd hear voices that were accusing me, saying how dare you think you can possibly be a part of this lovely home, you just keep your mouth shut and stay away.

I used to have the same dream – I don't any more. I would see all the people I knew, they would be beside me and all of a sudden I would start going up, getting higher and higher and higher and I couldn't get down to them. I was fighting for all I was worth to get down from whatever was lifting me up and I couldn't. I could see what was going on down below me and I wanted to be part of it.

I was grateful that she didn't send me to a psychiatrist. It would have been disastrous. Having been in the mental ward, I was terrified of going back there. Now I am an adult, I can cope with it, but even today if I walk into a hospital and there is a smell, or I hear a sound, I immediately get really alarmed.

If I'd been given a label when I was a kid, it would have been one label too many to carry around with me. It would have been the straw and the camel's back. I was already the odd guy who was adopted, with one parent and dyslexia.

I am still not convinced by psychiatrists but I am very happy with the one I have. He is very open and understanding to alternative methods. He's not anal about filling in all the boxes. There is a trust between the two of us.

Jeannie and Gordon Mackenzie have written their story in a book, As If I Were a Real Boy, *published by BAAF in 2011.*

Ellen and Bob, Jenny and Daniel

Ellen and Bob (not their real names) decided to adopt when they were both in their late 40s. Their birth children were grown up and had left home. They especially wanted to adopt older children who needed a family. Siblings Jenny and Daniel came to live with them in 1994, aged eight and six. The children's early lives had been truly horrendous, but Ellen and Bob were told very little about their background by social services. This is their story in their own words.

We turned down three children before we met Jenny and Daniel. One was a baby with AIDS, with only 10 years to live. One was a three-year-old whose mother kept trying to sell him, and there were two little girls who had been horrifically sexually abused. It tore us apart emotionally to have to make the decision not to adopt any of them, especially as we had been on the adoption waiting list for about three years, and we were in our late 40s, so time wasn't on our side. But finally our heads ruled our hearts – we knew that we couldn't manage their level of difficulties. We didn't meet any of them – we had decided we wouldn't unless we were going to go through with the adoption. It would have heaped even more rejection on them if we'd met them and then said no.

We were also turned down ourselves by one local authority, which, after meeting us, wrote to say we were 'too high flyers'. We don't think we are. We felt rejected then.

When we read the information we were sent about Jenny and Daniel, we talked long and hard and decided that maybe we could manage their level of damage.

But from the very beginning we weren't given the true facts about the children's history and birth family. The local authority only gave us the bare bones of the picture. We still have the children's adoption forms and they bear little resemblance to what we later experienced and learned.

The local vicar and his wife, in the area where they lived with their birth family, used to take the children in and bathe and feed them. Even in an inner city school they apparently stood out as being dirty, lice-ridden and hungry. The vicar found out that the family food was being eaten by their father.

We contacted the vicar after the children moved in with us, to try to make sense of their background, and he wrote to us with a lot of new information. His description of the flat where they lived was totally different from anything in the social services report. It was horrendous. All we had been told was that both parents had severe learning difficulties.

We learned that, when she went to nursery school, Jenny alerted the social services to some sort of sexual abuse by her father, usually at bath time. Her mother, it later turned out, was also involved. The children were then put on the at-risk register and their father was removed from the family, but he returned when there was insufficient evidence to bring a case against him.

There were no boundaries in the family. Sexual behaviour went on openly in the presence of the children, and not just between the parents. Both parents blamed Jenny for the father being removed, and they punished her by not washing, dressing or feeding her properly and ignoring her. The father then started to turn his sexual attentions towards Daniel. When the mother died very suddenly, the children and their father moved in with the father's brother and his wife and their two young children. Social services had said that Jenny must never be left alone with her uncle – he had been in a high security prison – but of course while she was living with him she was left alone with him.

Later, when the children had been removed into foster care, both the father and his brother were imprisoned for repeatedly raping the brother's wife, who had schizophrenia.

Social services attempted to keep the family together. They put the father and children in a hostel where they tried to teach the father how to parent them, but he wasn't interested; he said he wanted them to be adopted, so they put them into foster care for nine months. That's when we met them. But even there they hadn't been safe. Their foster carer treated them badly and was later removed from the local authority list.

At the court adoption hearing their birth father wasn't given any visiting rights. He died a few years ago.

We met Jenny and Daniel about four or five times before they came to live with us. When they moved in, they arrived with just two black bin liners full of shabby second-hand clothes, and an elderly white rabbit. The family flat had been full of animals – dogs and cats and rabbits.

They had no experience of a "normal" family and that's what we gave them, and they took to it. We provided routine, boundaries, food – they'd eat anything and lots of it. We did all the things you do with children that they'd never had the opportunity to do before. They loved the pretend play, the bedtime stories, playing not destroying, and sharing – all very basic things. We had a dog and cats, and lots of people coming into the house. The dog claimed them and they claimed him.

They were always very affectionate and physical. But they weren't easy to live with. Daniel had huge temper tantrums that weren't age-appropriate – it was helpful to remember that our eldest birth son used to have them too, and we dealt with Daniel's behaviour in the same way. Jenny was also very angry. She used to scream and scream that she hated us. Danny and I would listen to Mozart while this went on – he used to say, 'She doesn't mean it, Mum'. He was frightened we would send them back.

They shouted and screamed and rampaged through the house. But neither of them ever attempted to physically harm us or each other. They never damaged anything of ours, and the house is full of breakable stuff. Jenny always wrote sorry notes. They were both loving and gentle to the dog and the cats. A friend built their rabbit a new hutch and we would clean it out together at weekends.

We discovered that the head teacher of our local primary school knew the vicar who had looked after the children when they lived with their birth family. We met him and he agreed to take them. The school was amazing. They hung onto them despite all their stealing and anti-social and inappropriate behaviours. To begin with Jenny would just sit and bang her head on the desk most of the day. Neither of them could read or write or had any boundaries. But the school never wavered. We wouldn't have managed through those school years without that support, and also the support of the comprehensive schools they later attended – they went to different schools – where their behaviour was still far from "normal".

We were always aware they would find life a struggle because of the effects of their early childhood. Although we never thought of them as having any kind of mental disorder, they always responded to a good therapist. Thanks to our adoption worker we received some financial support from the local authority, which was hugely helpful for buying essentials, like beds, but also went towards paying for them to have therapy.

We found a highly qualified and renowned child psychotherapist and Jenny and Daniel both saw her separately for several years. She was also very supportive to both of us. Her advice to us was to ignore 95 per cent of the behaviour. That was tremendously helpful at times. The local authority paid but we still had to make the two hour journey each way.

Neither Jenny nor Daniel ever said they didn't want to go. They started off just enjoying the games they played in the sessions, and then they realised that she was on their side. We totally believed they would both benefit, knowing that we didn't have the skills to help them in that way. We witnessed the gradual changes in how they talked about their problems and maybe we learnt to give them the opportunity to talk about them too. When they were 13 they moved on to a recommended NHS psychotherapist who worked with young adults. The journey was shorter and they went by train.

Daniel's done a wonderful job in moving on from the past. When he was aged 10 he decided he wanted to change his first name. We went through all the formalities. He chose new names that he liked. They also both made the decision for themselves that they wanted to be formally adopted by us.

When they first came we had a live-in au pair, but the children were awful to her and she understandably couldn't cope. Because of the type of work I do, after a few months I was able to work from home. That solved the problem. My office door was always open and often they did their homework while I worked in the same room.

A close family friend got on really well with the children. She had a small place in the country and finally moved there permanently. The children stayed with her for the occasional weekend. Later they stayed for a week, or for a fortnight in the school holidays. They truly loved the freedom of the countryside and it gave us a much needed opportunity to have some time together on our own at home without any emotional wars – a time when we could regain some sanity, knowing that the children were happy and well cared for.

Both children stole, from school, family friends, strangers and from us, for many years; they stopped doing it only quite recently. They never stole together. We never punished them for it, but objects and money had to be returned so we learned to be detectives.

I took Danny to see his birth mother's grave. Jenny didn't want to come. We took the pictures Daniel had drawn for her.

Jenny had been Daniel's mother figure, and to begin with he deferred to her about everything. We didn't try to stop him. Then one day he told her firmly that she wasn't his mother. You could see how difficult that was for her. That had been her role in life and now who was she? But I think that freed her to become the child that she was. She used to ask me: 'If I was your baby, where would my cot have been?' and I'd tell her and I'd describe the cot to her and we'd draw it.

Jenny made great strides. She learned to read and write and got a place at university, but she dropped out after a year. She has huge social problems. She struggles to make friends. She was always very lonely – as a child she couldn't get on with other girls. No one would share a tent with her on school camping trips. She didn't move back home after she dropped out of university. She's unemployed and shares a flat with a boyfriend. When I visit her, she still holds my hand. She's still a child in many ways.

Daniel still lives at home with us. He got a place at art college but also dropped out after a year. He now has a job at a local DIY superstore, and a girlfriend. He has always been more sociable than Jenny. He can chat. But he has a form of autism. He's quite obsessive. He's also emotionally very naive, very vulnerable. But he's good with numbers. Even when they were very young he knew which bus to take.

The emotional whirlwind was exhausting at times, and sometimes it seemed never-ending. It isn't over now, of course. We know we couldn't have done it when we were younger, or without the support of the children's schools, therapists and friends. We have never regretted it, but there have been times when we've been close to it – the times when they stole money from a close friend or from a work colleague, or when Jenny was screaming down the length of Los Angeles airport, 'You aren't even my real mum'. Then it was hard not to think, 'Why did we choose this?'

Jenny said to me recently, how could she ever match us? I do wonder if adoption creates another difficulty for children because it makes them glimpse what they can't achieve. But you have to look at all the good things – maybe they haven't achieved all we'd hoped for them and all they might have done if it wasn't for their early life. But if we hadn't adopted them, Daniel would probably have been in prison by now for some minor crime – he's the kind of lad who gets caught by the police because he's not quick enough to run away. Jenny might have had three or four children by now. Neither of them drink or do drugs. Daniel once said, 'I know about unwanted babies. I was an unwanted baby and I struck lucky.'

We made a big difference to their lives. But we could never make up for the abandonment by their birth parents. You think when you adopt a child that love will make everything alright. But when children have had such a horrendous early life, love isn't enough. They need so much more, both practically and emotionally.

Ellen and Bob's advice to other adoptive parents is:

- Don't let your heart rule your head – be totally realistic about what you can manage before you embark on adoption.

- Ask lots of questions – try to find out all you can about the difficulties the child(ren) may bring with them from their early lives, so you know what to expect.

- Ignore 95 per cent of the behaviour.

- Don't try to do it all on your own – involve the school, friends, family, even pets.

- Get expert professional advice if you think it would help your child(ren) and they find it helpful – remember, it is supposed to help them, not you.

- Take time out – organise your lives so you can get time together away from the child(ren).

- Don't expect to be able to achieve the miraculous –
  love can do a lot but there are some hurts it cannot
  heal.

Angela and David, Charlotte and Jack

Angela and David (not their real names) decided to adopt when they found they were unable to have children themselves. They adopted Charlotte first, aged six months. Jack was four months old when they adopted him three years later.

The two children are very different. Jack has never been a problem. Charlotte was always more demanding, and her behaviour was much more difficult to manage. Then, when she was 15, she began to have violent, destructive rages if she was crossed or challenged.

Angela: Charlotte wasn't easy as a child. If she wanted to do something you couldn't get her to change her mind. She always had to have the last word. She would get into terrible tantrums. You couldn't calm her down, and she couldn't calm herself down. We went on holiday once to Spain – she was aged three or four – and she cried all the way from the airport until we got home. She just screamed for hours. That would happen quite often. Then she'd just stop and go on as if nothing had happened.

David: For the first 15 years of her life she was fine. People would say she's an opinionated little girl but it wasn't a major issue. She was very bright, very sharp, but frustrated all the time. You very rarely won an argument with Charlotte. She's very black and white in her thinking. She wanted to dominate other people. She has a very good memory and reads a lot. She did well at school – she was a bit stroppy but she was in the top two per cent of her class at secondary school. She should have gone to university.

I think she wanted to be the best. At age 15 she decided if she couldn't be top of the top two per cent, she'd be the best in the gutter. And she was. She just stopped achieving at school and started a relationship with the brother of a friend and it all went downhill.

The violence of Charlotte's rages is completely out of proportion to what triggers them.

Angela: She throws crockery, breaks doors. She's ripped out the phone, and attacked us both physically. She's chased David out of the house with a knife. She's even jumped out of the car while it was moving. She's reported David to the police for attacking her. We've had the police round so often and she's really rude to them. She's run away several times. She once put herself into care for a week. Another time she ran away and slept in her boyfriend's car. But she never goes far away. She always stays in touch and comes back.

At the time, nothing exists apart from her opinion. It doesn't matter who she's hurting. She is right and you are wrong. It's like living on a volcano. She blows up about twice a month. She's either on a high or very low. She has had jobs and has done very well in them, but she only lasts a few months before she falls out with her employer and walks out.

We tried to get her to go to anger management classes but she refused. She won't even talk about her behaviour. We'd always say, 'Don't say sorry if you don't mean it'. We have heard the word sorry so many times and she doesn't learn from it. What can we do? We tell her, 'You are still our daughter and we still love you'.

Finally, David and Angela told Charlotte she couldn't come into the house any more. Social services found her a flat nearby, where she now lives with her partner, Mick. She recently gave birth to a little baby boy. Charlotte rages at Mick too, and won't let his mother and sisters have anything to do with the baby. The couple row constantly and violently and Angela and David step in to try to help, and to mediate between them.

David and Angela don't understand where the rages came from. They knew very little about either child's birth parents, and wonder now if they should have been told more.

David: When you see her at her worst, it's like she's got a mental problem, but I think that's a cop-out. Maybe if we'd managed to get treatment when the rages started, it would have been different. But whatever it is, it's seven years too late to go back and put it right. It could be in the genes. We know her father was violent; maybe he had the same sort of thing. We were told something but we weren't told enough. We'd need to know what he's like now, what her mother's like now.

Charlotte's mother already had one child by another father. She wanted to keep Charlotte. She put her into foster care and then took her back for a few weeks but she couldn't cope with having two very young children. She was very young herself, and she just didn't like Charlotte's father. We have a picture of her mother and sister. Her mother's a very beautiful woman. Charlotte looks just like her.

Angela: They've both always known they are adopted. Charlotte always said she was pleased she'd been told from the start. When she was aged six she stood up in class and said, 'I am Charlotte and I am adopted and I think I'm special'.

We did have the adoption worker come and see her a few times and chat to her and they said, 'If you're sure you want to contact your mother don't do it on your own. We will help you.' I spoke to Charlotte about it when she was pregnant, but she said she wasn't ready yet to contact her mother.

But having the baby seems to have opened Charlotte's eyes to the fact that she has a problem and that there may be serious consequences. She recently went to see her GP, and asked Angela to come with her.

Angela: The GP was brilliant. She's a new, young doctor and Charlotte gets on with her. She told her, 'I'm desperate, I know I have a problem and I need something to sort my problem out. I don't want my son taken away from me.' The GP has prescribed her antidepressants and has also arranged for her to have a thyroid test.

When she got pregnant she said she now had someone to love. And since she's had the baby, she's spoken about her birth mother not loving her. She had a big bust-up with Mick and I said it's not good for the baby, he may be taken away. She said her mother didn't want her and then she asked, 'Why didn't my mother want me?'. I told her that her mum wanted to give her a better life than she could.

She adores her granny – my mother. She's over 80 now. When they were little they'd visit her every Saturday and even now Charlotte will sit and chat with her for hours and ask her about the past. She would never do any harm to her. She said to me the other night she was worried about what will happen when Granny goes and she said, 'I can't imagine what I'd do when you and Dad go.'

When it's good we talk a lot. I love her desperately, and we can get on well. I'd spent the afternoon with her and later she texted me to thank me and to say she is so glad she has me and David and that we adopted her and that I'm her mum and 'not that woman who didn't want me'. I told her, 'Charlotte, you have been the best thing that happened to David and me,' and she laughed. Recently we've dropped the ban on her coming to the house, and I think she's loved that.

Jack is still living at home. Like David, he loves sport and physical fitness. He has a job at the local garden centre but plans to join the Forces.

David: If it had been just Jack it would have been a different story. It hasn't been easy for him. I think joining the Forces is his way of getting away. But Charlotte worships him. They get on well together and always have.

So how have they coped?

Angela: I wouldn't have managed without David. He is good with Charlotte, and firm. I hold back and do the softer bit. It helps that we've never argued over it. We've always supported each other. Jack has been a rock throughout all this. He's mediated between us and Charlotte when things were really bad.

David: We've been married 30 years, and we've never argued. We have very good friends. Everybody knows about our problems and some have witnessed Charlotte at her worst. They've come round and seen us standing with all the broken crockery all round us. I play a lot of sport and run my own business. We've got a lot of interests and we haven't let it take over our life. But you are worrying all the time about the next phone call. We're worried now about leaving her for a week when we go on holiday. But, for all that's happened, we'd do the same thing again.

Postscript
Since she's been on antidepressants, Charlotte's behaviour has completely changed. She's much calmer,

SECTION II

says she feels happy for the first time for years, and is no longer having rages. She is now spending two days a week with Angela and David and Jack, and drops in frequently at other times. Angela and David have no idea what's caused the transformation – they're not even sure it will last. Maybe the antidepressants are relieving some longstanding, underlying condition linked to the rages; maybe Charlotte is learning to take care of herself and other people. Perhaps, having taken the decision to ask for help, she is now feeling more in control of her own life. Probably it's a combination of all of these.

Angela: She's like a different person – although it's early days; we're waiting to see what happens. She's lovely with the baby, and with her partner. She says she feels like she did when she was a little girl before all the trouble, and she wishes she'd taken our advice and got help sooner. But she also knows she had to work this out and make the decision for herself.

Angela and David's advice to other adoptive parents is:

- Try to find out everything that is known about your child's birth family and background – it may help you understand their behaviour.

- Support each other – understand how each of you contributes something important to your child's happiness and wellbeing.

- Don't let your problems with your child take over your

lives – keep working, going out, seeing friends.

● Don't try to keep your problems hidden from friends and family – you have nothing to be ashamed of and you will need their support.

● Be there for your child – would you disown or abandon your birth child?

● Don't immediately look for a mental disorder explanation – it may stop you looking for other solutions.

● Set clear boundaries (for you and for your child) and keep to them.

● Keep telling your child you love her/him – she or he needs to know this and one day she or he will hear you.

Abby and Jim, Harry and April

SECTION II

Abby and Jim decided to adopt when they found they were unable to have their own children. It wasn't an immediate decision.

Abby: For several years after the infertility treatment didn't work out, we thought, 'It's OK, it's meant to be and we're happy as we are.' Then we began to think, 'Maybe we're not so happy', and we started looking into adoption. We realised we still felt we wanted to be a family.

In the end, it was a deliberate choice to adopt older children, rather than a baby. I had always thought the younger the better: that seemed to be what all the information was saying. But then I got scared about the developmental uncertainty. I work professionally with young children so I know a lot about the risks. If you adopt a baby you don't know what developmental damage may have already been done pre-birth – that became much more of a factor than we first thought – so we settled on an age range between three and five years.

We always wanted two children rather than one, and we wanted two siblings together. We felt they would support each other.

Jim: We'd had such an unhappy time with the IVF treatment and we thought, if the child isn't genetically ours, then what's the point? But over time we realised we had good relationships with our nephews and nieces who aren't genetically ours. Then we both suddenly found ourselves thinking we did want to adopt, without really knowing how it happened.

They contacted the local authorities in their area who responded that they either didn't want white adoptive families or (less dismissively) currently didn't need them. So they got in touch with Coram, the national children's charity, which runs a voluntary adoption service. The children it places tend to come from more difficult backgrounds and to be harder to find adoptive parents for.

Abby: They were amazing. They were welcoming and interested in us right from the start, and very professional.

Jim: We took part in an adoptive parent preparation group, which dispelled any sugar-coated notions we might have had straight away. We were allocated a Coram social worker who was very helpful and proactive. Looking at the magazines full of children needing homes is a pretty depressing experience. You learn to read between the lines.

We wanted children who were attached to each other and who had a good sense of humour. A lot of the children in the adoption magazines look very posed and unnatural. Harry and April looked somehow resilient.

Abby:　We weren't particularly concerned about mental disorder in the birth family, though we did make a conscious decision not to adopt children whose birth parent had schizophrenia, due to the known inherited risk. We didn't feel we could live through the teenage years worrying about cannabis smoking – it's a possible trigger for psychosis – or waiting for the first signs of the disorder. I know from my professional work how people's lives can be utterly devastated by severe mental disorders such as schizophrenia, and I didn't feel comfortable even with the relatively small genetic risk.

Siblings Harry and April came to live with Abby and Jim in December 2007. Harry was nearly five, and April nearly four. Their home life had been very difficult. They had been living with a foster carer for about 15 months after being removed from their birth parents because of severe neglect. Both their parents suffered from depression and personality disorder; both used drugs and alcohol. The children had been raised in one room, which they shared with their parents, and rarely if ever went outside, so they were physically under-developed and weak, mainly through lack of opportunity to run around. When they came to live with the foster carer, they weren't toilet trained, had never learned to eat with a knife and fork, and had been fed a diet of yoghurt and potato waffles. Harry's behaviour suggested he had been physically hurt.

Abby and Jim were given a lot of information about Harry and April's family background and upbringing. They had psychiatric reports on the children, the report from the guardian ad litem (now the Children's Guardian) and the foster carer's report.

Abby: Both parents had mental health issues. Both had actively threatened suicide in front of the children. Their mother very probably drank through both pregnancies. The mother's family was also very dysfunctional. She had been abused by her step-father and the mother didn't believe her and kicked her out aged 16. The father's family was more "normal", but probably quite deprived.

Social services had sent them on parenting courses to try to improve their parenting skills but it didn't help and in the end the police took the children away. Social services finally admitted they had left them with their birth parents about 18 months too long. The guardian ad litem's report was really difficult reading. The children turned up at the foster carers with just one shopping bag of possessions. April had no toys of her own. We think Harry acted as a proxy carer for April and he got more of the abuse and shouting. She was just left in her buggy.

But there's always stuff you don't know. We think the foster carer underplayed Harry's behavioural problems.

We didn't get any specific advice from Coram about the effects of parental mental health problems, although we think it was covered in the preparation group we attended. However, I read up about it quite a bit, and also discussed it with a colleague at work. We were slightly perturbed when the possibility of the birth father having schizophrenia was raised at one point. I think the birth mother raised it. But she also claimed that her brother had Asperger's Syndrome and she was thought to fabricate things. We were fortunate to have access to detailed psychiatric reports on both parents and there was absolutely no mention of psychosis or anything else that sounded like schizophrenia.

We did know that both parents had a personality disorder diagnosis, but we knew this could arise from difficulties in their own childhoods. We regarded this as more of an environmentally-caused mental health problem than one that might be inherited. Jim has suffered depression several times and has managed to recover with support, so the possibility of depression didn't really concern us. Also, depression and anxiety are very common in people with personality disorders, so we felt this was the possible cause, rather than genetics.

Jim: We met the parents. We thought it was a good thing to do. It was difficult but worth it because now we can tell the kids, 'Yes, we have met your mum and dad,' and it's a link for them. They weren't monsters; they didn't have two heads. They talked about the kids with affection. We can at least tell the kids they cared enough to turn up and weren't angry and didn't freak out and we have some photos of the meeting to show them when they're older.

You had to feel sorry for them, to have had two children and then for them to be taken away.

Abby: We have letterbox contact with the parents once a year but we never hear anything back from them. Last year Harry asked us to tell them, 'I still love you' and April wanted us to write, 'Why didn't you feed us?'

Once they decided they would adopt Harry and April, 'it was like a runaway train,' says Abby. The foster carer needed to go into hospital, and they found themselves with ten days to prepare for the children to come to live with them, just before Christmas – and they were renovating the house at the same time.

Jim: The poor little things were obviously terrified but they had been well prepared and were super keen and excited about it. When we went to collect them from the foster carer, you could hear their little feet running along the corridor and them shouting, 'Here's our new mum and dad!' They made it very easy for us, though it must have been a big wrench to leave the foster carer.

Abby: She had done a lot of really good work with them. She'd got them toilet trained and sleeping through the night and got them used to a normal diet and normal daily routine. April evidently had some physical developmental delay, but no obvious emotional difficulties. Harry was very emotionally volatile, right from the start.

Abby: Initially he was very needy of attention. You'd be playing with him in one room and go to put the kettle on in the kitchen and before you'd taken ten paces he would start to bellow. We were told to get him into school as soon as possible so he went to the local school for the end of the Christmas term and he was clearly struggling, so Coram told us to take him out and give him more "mummy time" – he needed longer to establish a secure attachment to us. But it was ages before he would play in a room on his own for any length of time.

Most of the time he seems completely happy. He's bonded with our families, he's very enthusiastic, very loving, enjoys lots of things, and then suddenly he has these thunderstorms out of the blue sky.

It took us a while to identify the triggers. He seems emotionally wired to react to small things. If he thinks you have told him off, or he's not getting his own way, or he thinks April's getting something he isn't, he gets incredibly angry, incredibly quickly.

Jim: He rants and raves. There's lots of angry talking. He throws things too, and breaks things – he tends to target April's stuff. He gets very argumentative about totally random things. The corners he chooses to fight from are so ludicrous but that doesn't seem to occur to him. He will argue that black is white. He can also be physically violent. He'll kick and hit Abby, but not me, and he'll kick out at April too if she walks past when he's having one of his tantrums. She doesn't seem to be able to stay away. She's concerned for him, but she puts herself in his way.

Abby: It can go on for five or ten minutes or it can go on for an hour or more. Then it just stops. After a really big one he's pretty tired and sad and wrung out, and sometimes he's quite sorry, but not always. Although the other day he came spontaneously and apologised for something and it was very genuine and heart-felt. But most of the time he can't accept that he's done wrong, even when he seems to have calmed down.

He doesn't have the tantrums at school but he has some problems socialising. He gets easily upset if he feels a social situation isn't going his way. He likes to be in control of games. He finds it hard to go along with how other children play. He likes to be in charge and he'll rewrite the rules to suit himself. He does have some friends, but he doesn't seem that bothered about playing with them. He'll say no one likes him, but then when you get to the school gates he'll just ignore the other children in the playground.

April is quite different. She seemed almost to be in shock for the first three months. She was very quiet and smiley. It was like she was on "Planet La-La". Developmentally she is very small for her age. She's seven now and looks about five. Her behaviour is also like a much younger child's and her language is still quite immature. When she first came she was very slim and bendy, she hated walking anywhere, but she's doing ballet and modern dance and swimming and she's a lot stronger now.

She does have some problems with making friends. Other children didn't want to play with her because she always wanted to play families and to be the baby. She is also very physical – she tends to go up to other people and hug them, and not all children feel comfortable with that. She'll hug her friends and hug Harry, and she loves being squeezed and hugged herself. She also cries very easily. But unlike Harry she doesn't get cross – although she has started to get a little bit cross lately, so I think she's coming down from La-La land.

Initially she also had a tendency to be uninhibited about her attachments. She was very trusting – she'd go off with people she doesn't know. We had to do a lot of work on that, teaching her that she needs to see us as

her main attachment figures and refer everything back
to us.

*Harry is having sessions with a child psychotherapist
at the Tavistock Centre in London. Initially he saw the
psychotherapist with Abby and Jim because he wouldn't
co-operate on his own, but he seems much more
comfortable about the sessions now.*

Abby: Harry went through a very difficult period last October
and that was when we asked for a referral to the
Tavistock. He didn't want to go at first. He wouldn't talk
to the therapist and hid under the furniture. We ended
up offering him a financial reward to get him to go. But
now he's enjoying it so much I think we'll be stopping
that. They work with him on his feelings and emotions
and helping him understand them better. He enjoys the
attention.

Jim: We knew there were going to be some problems, and
we have to remind ourselves that Harry doesn't want to
be like this. He is just as much a victim of his behaviour
as we are. We've tried to help him understand why he
gets like this, that it isn't all his fault and it's because of
what happened in his early life. He is remarkably resilient
to have survived his early childhood and his attachment
to us is very deep. He does still sometimes have that
needy, anxious attachment behaviour but not often now.
In the holidays he goes off to Beavers and Cubs and
holiday club and he's fine. We've never been called in
because there's a problem.

*Abby and Jim are still much less concerned about
the parents' mental health histories and the possible
implications than about the emotional wellbeing of*

the children now, and the impact of their early life experiences.

Abby: Overall, we feel that the main effect of the parents' mental health problems was the poor parenting and neglect that the children suffered. It is extremely difficult to tease out any specific additional effects on the children's current and possible future difficulties. They clearly witnessed events – suicide attempts or preparations for suicide attempts – that are likely to have had an impact on their emotional wellbeing. April used to play games that involved taking pretend tablets. She always seemed quite happy during these games and certainly didn't seem to be acting out any suicide attempt, but we still found it worrying and discouraged it. She occasionally still does it but we tell her, 'No, we don't play with tablets' and she stops.

April may have some mild developmental delays due to her mother's alcohol intake during pregnancy – she has immature language, poor attention and concentration, poor motor co-ordination and immature social skills, all of which could be due to Foetal Alcohol Spectrum Disorder. Harry has had more emotional difficulties due to his early experiences – again, it's hard to say if this is due to the birth parents' mental health problems, but the domestic violence they witnessed, the inconsistent parenting, the regular disappearance of one or other parent, alcohol abuse and general neglect are just as likely to be the causes.

So the parents' mental health has definitely affected the children, but our feeling is that it's all so intertwined with the poor parenting and alcohol abuse that you can't be specific about its effects.

Currently we don't worry about the inheritance of

SECTION II

97

mental health issues. We are much more preoccupied with helping Harry with his emotional health now, and with April's development in order to give them the best chance for the future.

Abby and Jim's advice to other adoptive parents is:

- Seek help and advice: we didn't complete the legal part of the adoption process for 18 months because it meant we could still get a lot of support from our social worker. We really benefited from the help we got from Coram, and from attending the Coram parenting group. Your experience is so completely different from that of most birth parents you meet. At the Coram group you can see how other couples are coping with their difficulties – it meant we could go home and say to ourselves, at least we haven't got that problem! It puts the difficulties you're having into perspective and also the other parents understand what you are talking about. If you talk to other people with kids, they'll say, 'Oh, they all do that', and maybe they do, but not to the same extreme. There's a different quality to Harry's behaviour.

- Get as much information about the children as you can before you make your decision to adopt: we were given good information about the children in the pre-matching period. I don't feel that things were hidden from us or that we were in any way tricked into taking them. We had good information, we made our decision, and we knew what the likely challenges would be.

- Be completely honest with yourselves and with other people: you are doing the biggest thing you'll ever do in your life. There is no point in pulling the wool over your own or anyone's eyes. We were given a list of all the horrific things an adopted child might have been through and the sorts of problems and disabilities they might have. Be totally realistic about what you can handle. Once you have made the decision – that is it. You wouldn't want to send the child back.

SECTION II

References

Dozier M, Lindheim O, Lewis E, Bick J, Bernard K and Peloso E (2009) 'Effects of a foster parent training program on young children's attachment behaviors: preliminary evidence from a randomized clinical trial', *Child and Adolescent Social Work*, 26, pp 321–332

Glaser D (2000) 'Child abuse and neglect and the brain: a review', *Journal of Child Psychology & Psychiatry*, 41:1, pp 97–116

Gonzales-Pinto A, de Azua SR, Ibanez B, Otero-Cuesta S, Castro-Fornieles J, Graell-Berna M, Ugarte A, Parellada M, Moreno D, Soutullo C, Baeza I and Arango C (2011) 'Can positive family factors be protective against the development of psychosis?', *Psychiatric Research*, 186:1, pp 28–33

Gottesman II, Laursen TM, Bertelsen A and Mortensen PB (2010) 'Severe mental disorders in offspring with two psychiatrically ill parents', *Archives of General Psychiatry*, 67:3, pp 252–257

Greig A, Minnis H, Millward R, Sinclair C, Kennedy E, Towlson K, Reid W and Hill J (2008) 'Relationships and learning: a review and investigation of narrative coherence in looked-after children in primary school', *Educational Psychology in Practice*, 24:1, pp 13–27

Howard JA, Smith SL and Ryan SD (2004) 'A comparative study of child welfare adoptions with other types of adopted children and birth children', *Adoption Quarterly*, 7:3, pp 1–30

Keyes MA, Sharma A, Elkins IJ, Iacono WG and McGue M (2008) 'The mental health of US adolescents adopted in infancy', *Archives of Pediatrics and Adolescent Medicine*, 162:5, pp 419–425

Meltzer H, Corbin T, Gatward R, Goodman R and Ford T (2002) *The Mental Health of Young People Looked After by Local Authorities in England*, London: Office for National Statistics

Rethink (2008) *The Mental Health Act: Essential information for parents and carers*, London: Rethink. Available at: www.rethink.org.

Tarren-Sweeney M (2008) 'Retrospective and concurrent predictors of the mental health of children in care', *Children and Youth Services Review*, 30:1, pp 1–25

Tienari P, Wynne LC, Sorri A, Lahti I, Laksy K, Moring J, Naarala M, Nieminen P and Wahlberg KE (2004) 'Genotype–environment interaction in schizophrenia-spectrum disorder: long-term follow-up study of Finnish adoptees', *British Journal of Psychiatry*, 184, pp 216–222

Uher R and McGuffin P (2008) *Genetics of Mental Ill-Health in Children and Adults and Interaction of Genes with Social Factors*, State-of-Science Review: SR-B1, Foresight Mental Capital Project, London: Government Office for Science

van Os J, Kenis G and Rutten BP (2010) 'The environment and schizophrenia', *Nature*, 468:7321, pp 203–212

Wicks S, Hjern A and Dalman C (2010) 'Social risk or genetic liability for psychosis? A study of children born in Sweden and reared by adoptive parents', *American Journal of Psychiatry*, 167:10, pp 1240–1246

Wynne LC, Tienari P, Nieminen P, Sorri A, Lahti I, Moring J, Naarala M, Läksy K, Wahlberg KE and Miettunen J (2006) 'I. Genotype–environment interaction in the schizophrenia spectrum: genetic liability and global family ratings in the Finnish Adoption Study', *Family Process*, 45:4, pp 419–434

Useful organisations

YoungMinds
Source of useful information on all matters concerning the mental health of children and young people, and families. Publishes leaflets about and for children and young people with mental health problems and also runs a telephone helpline for parents.
Suite 11, Baden Place
Crosby Row
London SE1 1YW
Parents' Helpline: 0808 802 5544
www.youngminds.org.uk

SCIE (Social Care Institute for Excellence)
A good source of research-based information on the care of children with mental/emotional problems and their families, including looked after, fostered and adopted children. It is intended for professionals working in child and family health and social care but the research and information could be helpful to families also.

Fifth floor, 2–4 Cockspur Street
London SW1Y 5BH
Tel: 020 7024 7650
www.scie.org.uk

The Tavistock and Portman NHS Foundation Trust

Based in London but reputedly the best mental health service for
specialist individual and family therapy for children, young people
and families. Its website is very good on all things mental health – for
adults, children, young people and families.

Tavistock Centre

120 Belsize Lane
London NW3 5BA
Tel: 020 7435 7111

Portman Clinic

Portman Clinic
8 Fitzjohn's Avenue
London NW3 5BA
Tel: 020 7794 8262
www.tavistockandportman.nhs.uk

The Big White Wall, run in association with the Tavistock, is a brilliant
website on mental and emotional health for children and young
people.
www.bigwhitewall.com

South London and Maudsley NHS Foundation Trust

Provides the widest range of NHS mental health services in the
UK, including care and treatment for those living in south London,
and specialist services for people from across the UK. Operates
from a number of sites in the south London area. The Trust's
Child and Adolescent Adoption and Fostering Service provides a
specialist service for young adopted and fostered people who are

experiencing difficulties.

South London and Maudsley tel: 020 3228 6000

www.slam.nhs.uk

Child and Adolescent Adoption and Fostering Service

The Michael Rutter Centre for Children and Young People

Maudsley Hospital

De Crespigny Park (off Denmark Hill)

London SE5 8AZ

Tel: 020 3228 2546

Royal College of Psychiatrists

A good source of factual, medical information and accessible leaflets explaining child and adolescent mental health and emotional problems, the help available to families through the NHS and how to access it.

17 Belgrave Square

London SW1X 8PG

Tel: 020 7235 2351

www.rcpsych.ac.uk/mentalhealthinfoforall/youngpeople.aspx

Mind

A national charity for people with mental health problems. The website includes a section for children and young people with leaflets and information and sources of support for children, young people and families. The site also has good generic information about the range of mental and emotional disorders and treatments. Local Mind associations may also run specialist children and young people's mental health groups and projects.

15–19 Broadway

Stratford

London E15 4BQ

Tel: 020 8519 2122

www.mind.org.uk

BAAF

The leading UK-wide membership organisation for all those concerned with adoption, fostering and child care issues. BAAF provides advice, information and training to social workers and other practitioners, and publishes a wide range of books for workers, parents, carers and children on adoption, fostering and child care.

Head Office
Saffron House
6–10 Kirby Street
London EC1N 8TS
Tel: 020 7421 2600
www.baaf.org.uk

BAAF Cymru
7 Cleeve House
Lambourne Crescent
Cardiff
CF14 5GP
Tel: 029 2076 1155

BAAF Northern Ireland
Botanic House
1–5 Botanic Avenue
Belfast BT7 1JG
Tel: 028 9031 5494

BAAF Scotland
113 Rose Street
Edinburgh EH2 3DT
Tel: 0131 226 9270

Coram

An adoption agency based in London and the South East with particular expertise in placing children from troubled family backgrounds. Coram also offers specialist one-to-one and group parenting support, and "life education" learning support for parents.
49 Mecklenburgh Square
London WC1N 2QA
Tel: 020 7520 0300
www.coram.org.uk

Family Lives (formerly Parentline Plus)

A national charity which provides help and support to family members in all aspects of family life, including parenting, education, running a household, relationships and health.
CAN Mezzanine
49–51 East Road
London N1 6AH
Tel: 020 7553 3080
www.familylives.org.uk/

Direct.gov.uk

A government website which provides a useful first point of information on parenting in general, including benefits entitlements and information about adoption and fostering.
www.direct.gov.uk/en/Parents/index.htm